CASS SERIES ON POLITICS AND MILITARY AFFAIRS IN THE TWENTIETH CENTURY

LEON TROTSKY
AND THE
ART OF INSURRECTION
1905–1917

LEON TROTSKY
AND THE
ART OF INSURRECTION
1905–1917

HAROLD WALTER NELSON
U.S. Army War College

FRANK CASS

First published 1988 in Great Britain by
FRANK CASS AND COMPANY LIMITED
Gainsborough House, 11 Gainsborough Road,
London E11 1RS, England

and in the United States of America by
FRANK CASS AND COMPANY LIMITED
c/o Biblio Distribution Centre
81 Adams Drive, P.O. Box 327, Totowa, N.J. 07511

Copyright © 1988 Harold Walter Nelson

British Library Cataloguing in Publication Data

Nelson, Harold Walter
    Leon Trotsky and the art of insurrection
    1905-1917
    1. Soviet Union—History—Nicholas II,
    1894–1917   2. Soviet Union—Politics
    and government—1894-1917
    I. Title
    947.08'3   DK262

    ISBN 0-7146-3272-4 (cased)
    ISBN 0-7146-4065-4 (paper)

Library of Congress Cataloging-in-Publication Data

Nelson, Harold W.
    Leon Trotsky and the art of insurrection,
    1905–1917.

    Originally presented as the author's thesis
    (doctoral)
      Bibliography: p.
      Includes index.
      1. Trotsky, Leon, 1879–1940—Knowledge—Military
    art and science. 2. Soviet Union—History—
    Nicholas II, 1894–1917—Historiography. 3. Soviet
    Union—History, Military—1801–1917. I. Title.
    DK254.T6N45   1987   947.084'092'4   87-14164
    ISBN 0-7146-3272-4 (cased)
    ISBN 0-7146-4065-4 (paper)

Printed and bound in Great Britain by
A. Wheaton & Co. Ltd, Exeter

Contents

MAP

Note on Transliteration

There is no entirely satisfactory solution to the problem of transliterating names and words from Russian to English. I have followed the Library of Congress system with a few exceptions. The most obvious of these is exemplified in the title and in all subsequent references, where I have written "Trotsky", following customary English usage, rather than using the proper transliteration – Trotskii.

Acknowledgments

This work began as a doctoral dissertation more than a decade ago. Each passing year brought new support that I can now gratefully acknowledge. Throughout, I have been simultaneously pursuing academic interests and a military career – an endeavor that often posed formidable challenges. Since military commitments always came first, I can thank military men who reduced obstacles to my academic aspirations and scholars who encouraged my halting efforts.

Tom Griess, Bill Stofft, and Reg Shrader head the military ranks because they found places for me to teach at the Military Academy (West Point), the Command and General Staff College (Fort Leavenworth), and the Army War College (Carlisle Barracks). These teaching assignments allowed me to improve my knowledge of Soviet affairs, revolutionary theory, and military thought. At the same time, I was in the midst of stimulating colleagues and students who kept me abreast of military developments and convinced me that a monograph addressing the organization of revolutionary violence had more than passing relevance. Mike Krause, Bob Frank, Bob Doughty, and Rupert Pate were the colleagues who tirelessly shared burdens and provided inspiration when my research lagged. Some who were captains when this project began are now colonels. They obviously inspired many others in their careers dedicated to teaching an army.

Bill Rosenberg, John Shy, and Roman Szporluk – professors at the University of Michigan – head the list of patient scholars. They first captured me with their gifted teaching and then guided me through the complex joys of research and writing. When their interest began to bear fruit, Jay Luvaas and Michael Handel – professors at the Army War College – encouraged me to make the product into a finished work.

Anyone who uses his "free time" to write could not do so without remarkable family support. My wife, Janet, has stoically set up housekeeping in seven new places as this book progressed. In each instance, and in our everyday lives, she took on added tasks so that I could read my dusty books and think my dusty thoughts. Our daughters, Karen and Catherine, have made similar adjustments. I could not have achieved my military career objectives, let alone pursued my academic interests, without their loving support.

With all this help applied over so many years, I should have produced a perfect monograph. I have not, and I acknowledge that fault as my own.

H.W.N.

CHAPTER ONE

Introduction

Revolutions need generals; men who study the problems of armed conflict, organize the resources of war, and inspire men in battle are indispensable in the revolutionary situation. Without their leadership the revolutionary enthusiasm of the masses will be dissipated without effecting change. The revolutionary leader fears that the old order will be able to defend itself against uncoordinated revolutionary action, leaving power in the withered hands of an outmoded social class. In a workers' revolution the title of "general" may be anathema, but the function must still be performed. This is not to say that revolutionary military leaders and conservative military leaders will be interchangeable. In the definition of the nature of the struggle, in the selection and use of resources, and in the methods of leadership the revolutionary "general" will differ dramatically from his enemy who defends the established order. The similarity is one of function rather than style.

This functional definition of revolutionary military leadership is essential in understanding Leon Trotsky's role in the Russian Revolution, for most of the confusion which impedes our ability to analyze effectively the part he played in the October coup springs from an unwillingness to reconstruct carefully the functional role which Trotsky played and the experiences which had prepared him to fill that role. Trotsky was one of the revolution's "generals".

Contemporaries perceived this, and historians in the West have been echoing them for more than fifty years, so why spend more time on the most famous of the Russian revolutionary generals? The answer is embarrassingly simple. Each word – "revolutionary" and "general" carries a heavy connotative burden, and when the first is used to modify the second the new term does not lend itself to easy definition. Most writers who have described and analysed Trotsky have concentrated on the revolutionary, evaluating his performance in terms of the Marxian model which seems to be the best standard. Others have concentrated on his performance as a general, using what our Soviet colleagues like to call "bourgeois standards and assumptions" to evaluate his actions. Confusion arises because he seems to measure up quite well on both scales. Trotsky stayed much closer to Marxian ideals than his antagonists in the period after Lenin's death, and he defeated the White forces by borrowing many of the techniques of "bourgeois" military theory. The pro-revolutionary historian is encouraged to discover that the Stalinist aberration was not inevitable, and the military historian is pleased to discover that Trotsky insisted on firm discipline while appreciating the fact that he enjoyed the advantage of interior lines. But these observations, while comforting, are misleading. In his formative years before 1917 Trotsky had effectively integrated the two standards of performance into one, and he came into the revolutionary situation prepared to use his talents to provide solutions to the problem of armed conflict which faced the revolutionary masses. He was a military revolutionary theorist.[1]

We cannot understand this aspect of Trotsky's contribution simply in terms of early twentieth century European Marxian revolutionary theory or in terms of the military theory of the time. In military revolutionary theory Trotsky was above all a Russian theorist, drawing on the traditions as well as the innovations of the Russian revolutionary left. We must recognize that Russian Marxist military history does not begin with the origins of the Red Army in 1918 or with Petrograd military committees of 1917. The first conference of Russian Social Democratic Labor Party Military Organizations met in October, 1906. Earlier that year, at the Fourth Party Congress in Stockholm, the delegates had given careful consideration to questions of partisan warfare and armed insurrection. Russian Marxists, especially Bolsheviks, were engaged in developing a revolutionary military doctrine which went far beyond that of Marx and Engels. When Trotsky began to write on military topics after the revolution of 1905 he was responding to this preoccupation with violent revolution which had seized the imagination of his Russian colleagues.

When he had additional opportunities to test and develop his thoughts on military subjects in the Balkan Wars and in World War I, he used this framework of revolutionary military thought as the foundation for his analysis. When he returned to Russia in 1917 he was equipped to apply these theories to do what they had always been intended to do: achieve victory for the proletarian revolution in Russia. As a "revolutionary general", Trotsky's theories could take him no further. When he assumed the post of Commissar of War before the Russian revolution had triggered the world revolution, he was forced to improvise.

The accounts of the brilliance of that improvisation are numerous,

2

and this study does not attempt to add to their number. Instead, it is devoted to that little-known area of Party history dealing with military questions. Trotsky's writings are used as the principal means of charting a course through the shifting theories and confusing polemics which fill the period from 1905 to 1917.

Trotsky supported himself by working as a journalist during most of this period. His numerous newspaper columns can be combined with his theoretical work to give a sufficient picture of Trotsky's progress as a student of military affairs. The bulk of Trotsky's written efforts were brought together in his published *Sochineniia* (*Collected Works*) in the mid-1920s.[2] Unlike many published items dealing with Trotsky, this collection is quite reliable. Checks of the newpapers to which Trotsky contributed revealed that virtually all of his articles were included in the *Sochineniia*. Those which were omitted have no bearing on this study. Textual comparisons of the original newspaper articles with the versions appearing in the *Sochineniia* reassures the researcher, for Trotsky's editors did not alter the content.[3]

Alterations of the historical record plague the student of Trotsky. Once the *Sochineniia* has been used to chart the course further research must be conducted cautiously. The accuracy of war correspondent Trotsky's impressions of military affairs can be gauged by comparing them with the observations of other military analysts. It is more difficult to judge Trotsky's contributions as a political activist who sought to organize and direct violent means to support a revolutionary cause.

Judgments in this area are central to an understanding of Trotsky's maturation as a theoretician, but sources lack trustworthiness. Modern Soviet scholarship has not yet restored Trotsky to the gallery of revolutionary leaders, so many otherwise excellent works produced by our Soviet contemporaries on the period 1905–17 are of little value. Much of Trotsky's retrospective work of the 1930s lacks objectivity in its treatment of the pre-revolutionary period, and works produced by Trotsky's supporters generally have the same flaw. Most of these biases were avoided by concentrating research efforts on materials produced before 1927.

Published document collections and extracts of party records still gave Trotsky his due in the first decade after the revolution, and memoirists did not fear retribution if they gave Trotsky a central place in their accounts of revolutionary events. These sources have been used to put Trotsky's thoughts and actions into context.

Context is an important aspect of this study. Trotsky's most competent biographer chose to omit discussion of military thought.[4]

3

There have been efforts to fill this obvious gap by surveying Trotsky's military thought throughout his lifetime,[5] but this survey approach fails to investigate the broader issues which shaped Trotsky's thinking on military subjects. Before 1918 he was interested in determining the proper relationship between organized violence and revolutionary victory. The Bolshevik success in 1917 resulted in a new set of military problems. Trotsky's solutions to those post-revolutionary problems cannot be lumped together with his approach to the revolutionary issues addressed here.

As we follow Trotsky through the period from 1905 through 1917 he emerges as a genuine revolutionary general – one who can lead and coordinate decisive revolutionary action. He comes to understand the problems of armed conflict which the revolution must solve, he gains an appreciation of the resources which the revolution can call upon to solve these problems, he develops schemes for organizing these resources for maximum effectiveness, and he discerns the factors which motivate the men who must fight to gain the revolutionary victory.

This process of growth began during the revolution of 1905. Trotsky was only twenty-five years old when he returned from exile to participate in the exciting long-awaited events following the clash between workers and soldiers in St. Petersburg on Bloody Sunday, 9(22) January 1905. However, his insights into the theories of revolution were remarkably well-developed.[6] Born Lev Davidovoch Bronstein on 26 October (7 November) 1879, he spent his early years in a small settlement near Kherson in the Ukraine. When he was old enough to begin his education he stayed with relatives, first in Gromokla, then in Odessa, and finally in Nikolaev, progressing through the *Realschule* regimen. The young Lev Davidovoch demonstrated the combination of studious habits and brilliant verbal skills that was to characterize the mature Trotsky, but the development of a revolutionary philosophy was not so straightforward.

Russia in the 1880s and 1890s was cleary ripe for change, and discussion of proper methods and direction of change was a common surreptitious pastime for schoolboys. Tolstoyan arguments initially attracted Lev Davidovoch, but these were soon replaced by *narodnik* notions. Vague socialist ideas were common fare in a small circle he joined in Nikolaev in 1896. The conflict between agrarian socialism and the relatively new ideas of Marx soon penetrated this circle, and by the spring of 1897 Lev Davidovoch considered himself a Marxist and had set about organizing the workers of Nikolaev.

This effort provided the first outlet for his journalistic skills and also led to his first arrest early in 1898. After nearly two years in prison he was finally sentenced without trial and ordered into four years of administrative exile in Siberia. He did not complete the sentence. In the summer of 1902 he escaped from his place of exile near Irkutsk and by October of that year he joined Lenin in London.

During his years in prison and in exile Trotsky had been able to study and write. His knowledge of revolutionary theories had developed rapidly, and his talents as a polemicist had become more sophisticated. Lenin and his colleagues capitalized upon these skills, and Trotsky's speeches and newspaper articles soon gained him the respect of prominent Russian Social Democrats in emigration. When factional infighting split the party in 1903 Trotsky had already become one of the principal spokesmen, but his inability to accept Lenin's theories weakened Trotsky's position. Trotsky opposed Lenin's concept of a tightly-controlled, centrally-directed party apparatus, fearing that it would stifle initiative within the party and deter popular support. Yet he was equally distressed with gradualist elements in the Menshevik faction advocating programs having no apparent revolutionary content. Trotsky found himself differing with almost everyone in 1904.

The revolutionary events of 1905 seemed to promise an end to all the theoretical hair-splitting of politics in emigration, and Trotsky eagerly returned to Russia in February, 1905. Throughout the spring and summer he engaged in clandestine activity, and in October he emerged in the St. Petersburg Soviet. This Council of elected representatives of the Petersburg workers lasted only fifty days, but before it was disbanded by the forces of reaction Trotsky had become its chairman. He was once again imprisoned, but Trotsky had established his position as a prominent Social Democrat committed to solving the problems preventing revolutionary success. One of the most difficult of these was the question of military power, and Trotsky seems to have realized that neither his family background and boyhood studies nor his previous revolutionary experience had prepared him to cope with this problem. He failed to solve it in 1905, and his failure had disastrous consequences for the revolution. In the years that followed he gave military matters careful attention, ultimately developing the skills he demonstrated in the triumph of 1917.

CHAPTER TWO

Trotsky's Analysis of the Lessons of 1905

To concentrate on Trotsky's development as a military theorist is not to isolate this aspect of his intellectual growth from all others. Leon Trotsky never concentrated his full attention on military matters; even as Commissar of War he found time for numerous intellectual pursuits which had virtually nothing to do with military affairs. Yet even though his study of war was not systematic, it can be analyzed systematically if it is viewed in the larger context of his "revolutionary development". Throughout his adult life Trotsky was attempting to improve his capability to discern and interact with the revolutionary forces of the moment. The bitter lessons of 1905 convinced him that the use of armed force was one of the revolutionary skills which had to be mastered, and from that time forward he consciously worked to understand the revolutionary implications of military conditions (and the military implications of revolutionary situations). As time passed he became more sophisticated in his analysis of military affairs, ultimately emerging as an innovative theorist. But throughout this process of self-development and education he was considering military problems in the broader context of the fundamental issue – the successful proletarian revolution.

This context is most important in understanding Trotsky's assessment of the military implications of the experiences of the St. Petersburg Soviet in the Revolution of 1905. In his early writings on the subject, Trotsky discussed the military situation as a source of lessons to be learned. The lessons he learned were important ones which he never discarded, but they were extremely general in application and were to become more fully articulated as a result of his later military experiences.

The fundamental military observation which Trotsky made after the 1905 revolution was that "the Russian Proletariat in December 1905 foundered, not on its own mistakes, but on a more real force: the bayonets of the peasant army".[1] This generalization was justified, for the army that was unable to defeat Japan's forces proved strong enough to suppress internal rebellion. Some units mutinied, but throughout the Russian Empire, in Europe and Asia, in cities and in villages, sufficient numbers of loyal troops responded to the tsar's call, moved to the critical points, and restored order. The government imposed martial law. As Trotsky wrote the army was enforcing martial law even though embers of revolution flared up into small isolated flames of violence. Officers and soldiers worked together against the revolutionaries. Execution squads performed their duties as the army employed nooses and bullets as well as bayonets to consolidate tsarist power.

Trotsky's observation that the revolution foundered on the bayonets of the peasant army serves as his thesis in his analysis of the military implications of the 1905 revolutionary experience. This analysis has several components, the most important of which are the inevitability of armed conflict, and the proper relationship between revolutionary armed might and the revolutionary masses during the conflict. While Trotsky's thinking on the first subject is clear and logical, his assessment of the last two is fuzzy and contradictory. All three must be examined carefully if his viewpoint of the military significance of 1905 is to be understood.

THE ROLE OF ARMED CONFLICT IN THE REVOLUTIONARY SITUATION

Trotsky's most detailed and explicit discussion of the inevitability of armed conflict between the forces of revolution and reaction occurred in his famous defense speech at the trial of the Soviet Deputies in October 1906. In this speech Trotsky argued that the Soviet of Workers' Deputies was not guilty of the charge of preparing an insurrection. Instead, he argued, the insurrection was unavoidable because of the situation, and the Soviet merely reflected the revolutionary enthusiasm of the masses. Trotsky pointed out that "the subject of an armed rising as such was not raised or discussed at any of our [the Soviet of Workers' Deputies] meetings",[2] but he went on to say that the only reason the subject never came up for explicit discussion was that everyone shared the opinion that an armed rising would eventually occur. Armed insurrection "was and remains a historical necessity in the process of the people's struggle against the military and the police state", and therefore "the idea of armed insurrection, if different forms but essentially the same, runs like a red thread from the very beginning of the Soviet's existence, through all the Soviet's discussions".[3]

The reasons for this belief in the inevitability of an armed clash are complex. Essentially Trotsky was arguing that the political strikes which had created the Soviets had also created a situation of fundamental political and social tension. Since the state resisted the demands of the workers as being contrary to the interests of the ruling class, it would inevitably marshal its forces of repression to insure its ability to govern. When this occurred there would be a clash between the armed forces of the state and the crowds of revolutionary workers who would have armed themselves to the best of their ability. The success of the revolution hinged upon the outcome of this conflict.

Stated in these general terms Trotsky's argument is a simple Marxian assessment of the revolutionary situation. Yet when we examine his ideas more carefully, we find that his experiences in 1905 had led him to develop some rather original conclusions concerning the inevitability of an armed clash. First, the development of the Soviet seemed to have important implications in the realm of the organized use of power by the revolutionary masses. In his Defense Speech Trotsky said:

> the Soviet, in the political strike which had created it, became nothing other than the organ of self-government of the revolutionary masses: an *organ of power*. It ruled the parts of the whole by the will of the whole. It was voluntarily obeyed. But inasmuch as the Soviet was the organized power of the overwhelming majority, it was inevitably compelled to use repressive measures against those elements among the masses who brought anarchy into its united ranks .... It was entitled to oppose its force to such elements.[4]

This power was the only truly legitimate power in existence during the period of revolutionary turmoil, and it gave the Soviet the right to organize an army. The organ which had the right to bring force to bear against those proletarian elements which defied its will clearly had the right and responsibility to organize forces to combat the illegitimate armed force of the state. Trotsky noted this distinction in legitimacy in his statement that

> The historical power which the prosecutor represents in this court is the organized violence of a minority over the majority. The new power, whose precursor was the Soviet, is the organized will of the majority calling the minority to order. In this distinction lies the Soviet's revolutionary right to existence, a right that stands above any legal or moral doubt.[5]

8

Having argued that the political strike gave life to a new, legitimate organ of power, Trotsky then pointed out that this gave rise to a new phase in the revolution's development in which "a titanic struggle for influence over the army begins between these two organs of power — the second stage of the popular insurrection".[6] This is the stage at which armed clash is inevitable:

> But is a peaceful transition of the army into the ranks of the revolution conceivable? No, it is not. Absolutism is not going to wait with folded arms for the army, freed from every corrupting influence, to become the friend of the people. Before all is lost, absolutism will take the initiative and launch an offensive.[7]

THE PRECONDITIONS FOR MILITARY VICTORY

While the armed clash was clearly inevitable, the preconditions for revolutionary success in that clash were not nearly so easy for Trotsky to define. The revolutionary "force equation" would seem to be quite easy to solve since there are only two elements involved: the strength of the military, and the strength of the revolutionary crowd. Obviously, whenever the latter is greater than the former revolutionary victory will follow. But it is just as obvious that both are variables, and the situation is further complicated by the possibility that "military strength" and "crowd strength" cannot easily be equated because they are not measured in the same terms. Trotsky's experiences in 1905 did not make it possible for him to solve this problem, but they attuned him to it, and he developed a remarkable ability to determine the quantity of the variables, the factors of which they are a function, and the manner in which they interact. He arrived at no definitive solution because he was unable to determine whether the strength of the crowd or the strength of the army was the critical variable.

Trotsky was most sure of himself in his analysis of military strength. His confidence showed in his rejection of Engels' writings on the subject of revolutionary conflict with modern (post-1870) armies.[8] Engels had postulated that the successful bourgeois revolution in Western Europe had fostered a new military opponent for future revolutionary movements. While the new armies relied on universal service to fill their ranks and thus were not themselves safe from revolutionary sentiments, this possible advantage for the revolutionaries was offset by technological innovations such as rapid-fire weapons, improved artillery, railroads, and telegraph communications which would allow the army of a modern state to respond to a revolutionary threat much more rapidly and with greater force. But Trotsky was not convinced. His statements clearly indicate that he shared Engels' appreciation of the military significance of modern technology:

> although the telegraph, the railway, and all the other attainments of modern technology may not serve Russian absolutism for cultural or economic ends, they are all the more essential to it for the purposes of repression. The railways and the telegraph are irreplaceable weapons for transferring troops from one end of the country to another, uniting and directing the administration's activities in suppressing sedition.[9]

But he pointed out that Engels

> overlooks the fact that a genuine mass rising inevitably presupposes a railway strike. Before the government can begin to transfer its armed forces it must – in ruthless combat with the striking personnel – seize the railway line and rolling stock, organize traffic, and restore the destroyed track and blown-up bridges. The best rifles and sharpest bayonets are not enough for all this .... Further, before proceeding to the transfer of armed forces, the government must know the state of affairs in the country. Telegraph speeds up information to an even greater extent that the railways speed up transport. But here again, a rising both presupposes and engenders a postal and telegraph strike.[10]

The military significance of the October strike had not been lost on Trotsky, and his estimate of the effect of strikes upon the ability of the government and its army to respond to the revolutionary threat was a well-founded revision of Engels' theory.

The question of the importance of the class composition of the army in determining the military response to the revolutionary threat was more difficult . Perhaps this was because at this stage of his career Trotsky had little first-hand knowledge of military life. His prison experience (1897–1902) had exposed him to the forces of repression, but because he had spent most of his term in solitary confinement or in rather lax Siberian exile he had not yet had a chance to meet the men behind the guns. His instincts told him that "people are not ruled by rifles, guns and battleships; in the final analysis, rifles, guns, and battleships are controlled by people".[11] Trotsky's ignorance of these people made it difficult for him to assess their responses to revolutionary situations.

Because Trotsky did not know how an army would respond, there is a fundamental ambivalence in his theory on the proper nature of the clash between the people and the army. He was quick to point out that the class nature of the army discerned by Engels "can become politically significant only when there is a direct confrontation between the army and the people"[12] and that "the army's political mood, that great unknown of every revolution, can be determined only in the process of a clash between the soldiers and the people".[13] Yet he seemed to be unsure whether the revolutionary masses should be most interested in fighting for the revolution or dying for it. Should the revolution attempt to turn the mob into an army or should it turn the army into a mob?

The distinction between fighting and dying highlights the problem in determining the strength of the masses in the revolutionary struggle. If the struggle is to be symmetrical, with military units of revolutionaries organized along conventional lines entering combat against similar organizations of the regular army, then the emphasis will be on fighting. But if the struggle is to be asymmetrical with the unarmed masses convincing the soldiers of the justice of their cause by demonstrating their willingness to take casualties, then the emphasis will be on dying. Events throughout 1905 culminating in the dramatic guerrilla warfare in Moscow during the December uprising made the "fighting" notion attractive to Trotsky, but it seems that the failure of the uprising drew him toward the "dying" approach as the only one which could assure revolutionary victory. Ultimately he drew upon both alternatives in organizing revolutionary violence, so both deserve careful consideration.

THE ROLE OF REVOLUTIONARY
FIGHTING ORGANIZATIONS

Trotsky made his first explicit appeal for a revolutionary fighting organization in a letter to *Iskra* published on 17 (30) March 1905.[14] Here he discussed the necessity of an armed uprising, stating that a critical point in revolutionary events would occur, at which time further progress toward a new order would be impossible without an uprising. In addition he wrote,

> We [the Russian Social Democratic Labor Party (RSDLP)] must organize the uprising .... Every committee must immediately organize a new agency: a military section which will prepare for the uprising .... We cannot organize the entire uprising, but we can make our presence felt, and where we are strong we can be ready.[15]

Organization of workers' militia units did not proceed rapidly, and Trotsky did not take cognizance of any genuine forces until the time of the October strike.[16] Then the organizations of workers who had armed themselves to defend the interests of the Soviet captured his attention, and he saw them as a vital force in the success of the Soviet of Workers' deputies. The print workers excited his interest:

> In sending their deputies to the Soviet, the print-workers formulated the tasks of the moment in even more resolute terms:
> "Recognizing the inadequacy of passive struggle and of the mere cessation of work, we resolve: to transform the army of the striking working class into a revolutionary army, that is to say, to organize detachments of armed workers forthwith. Let these detachments take care of arming the rest of the working masses, if necessary by raiding gun shops and confiscating arms from the police and troops wherever possible."
> Armed detachments of print-workers were extraordinarily successful in seizing the city's largest print shops for the printing of *Izvestia Soveta Rabochikh Deputatov* and performed invaluable services in organizing the postal and telegraph strike.[17]

In addition to being the first responsive and well-armed militia unit at the disposal of the St. Petersburg Soviet, the print-workers militia performed duties which were such that Trotsky noticed similarities to roles played by the armed units of the state:

> During general strikes, when all life came to a standstill, the old regime considered it a point of honor to continue printing its Government Gazette without interruption, and it did so under the protection of its troops. To this the Soviet opposed its armed workers' detachments, which ensured the publication of the revolution's own newspaper.[18]

Here we see the real appeal of symmetry — it allowed the forces of the Soviet to demonstrate the legitimacy which Trotsky had asserted was theirs when he spoke at his trial. If it had its own army the revolution could carry out all functions of government with impunity, having no fear of repression. The army of the revolution could meet the state's army on the field of battle, and behind this shield the revolutionary government would enjoy all the advantages of overt existence, including the right to publish its newspapers.

In direct contrast to this situation, the major disadvantage of the asymmetrical approach is seen in another of Trotsky's reflections on the status of the revolutionary press. In one of his more dramatic moods, Trotsky had written:

> We, armed only with our boundless faith in the gospel of international socialism, against the powerful enemy clad from head to foot in the armor of international militarism. Hiding in the nooks and crannies of "legal" society, we had declared war on autocracy, a struggle for life or death. What was our weapon? The word.[19]

Obviously Lenin had chosen wisely when he nicknamed Trotsky "Pero" (the Pen).[20] But in 1905 faith in the word alone seemed a bit utopian to Trotsky, and the David and Goliath mismatch that he evoked in this passage did not seem so attractive. If the revolution had powerful swords as well as powerful pens it would not be forced to hide in the nooks and crannies. It could defend its interests and confidently challenge the authority of the state. This was the possibility that made symmetry of fighting forces so attractive.

By November 1905 "symmetry" meant armed mobs for both sides. Black Hundreds had proliferated throughout Russia during the early autumn, and numerous bloody pogroms occurred. Since armed mobs threatened the revolution, it made even more sense to arm the workers. Thus the tendency toward fighting for survival and waging open warfare against the forces of repression was further reinforced. Trotsky did not overlook this implication:

> By arming itself against the Black Hundreds, the proletariat was automatically arming itself against Tsarist power. The government could not fail to understand this, and it raised the alarm. On November 8, the *Pravitel'stvennyi Vestnik* [Government Gazette] informed the public of facts which everyone knew anyway: namely, that the workers "have recently begun to arm themselves with revolvers, sporting guns, daggers," the government communiqué continued, "whose number, according to available information, reaches 6,000 men, there has been formed a so-called self-defense force or militia, numbering approximately 300 men, who walk the streets at night in groups of ten under the pretext of defence; their real aim, however, is to protect revolutionaries against arrest by the police or troops."[21]

Trotsky did not take issue with the assertion that the workers' militia did in fact protect the revolutionaries from arrest. The government clearly did not intend to tolerate further revolutionary activity, and the leaders of the Soviet led a risky existence during their short period of leadership.[22] As a result, it hardly can be considered odd that Trotsky had such admiration for the armed workers who risked arrest or death to provide security for the Soviet.

Trotsky went beyond mere statements of admiration. In a speech to the St. Petersburg Soviet on 5 (18) November he said:

> We must immediately proceed to organize and arm the workers for battle. You must form "fighting tens" with elected leaders at every plant, "hundreds" with other leaders and a commander over the "hundreds." You must develop discipline in these cells to such a high point that at any given moment the entire plant will march forward at the first call.[23]

Here he clearly called for a military organization prepared for open warfare with the gendarmes, cossacks, and soldiers of the autocracy. He stressed organization along hierarchical lines which would make the force responsive to the direction of the leadership, even though that leadership would be elected. The resulting organization would mobilize the masses, but it would do this through the aggressive leadership of the armed workers from plants which had sent deputies to the Soviet. Obviously a conventional conflict at the barricades could ensue.

Trotsky never reached the barricades in 1905. The inflammatory proclamations of the St. Petersburg Soviet led to his arrest along with the other leaders of the Soviet. But these arrests, together with the proclamations, provoked the armed rising which Trotsky had foreseen. It reached its greatest intensity in Moscow, and even though Trotsky was not a participant he analyzed the events of the uprising in sympathetic detail when he wrote about 1905. To put it simply, he was impressed by the guerrilla warfare which broke out in Moscow in December.

It was obvious that the armed bands of the Moscow Workers' organizations were too weak to defeat the garrison in pitched battle. Guerrilla warfare was an attractive alternative, and this became the accepted mode of fighting.

> As military operations began, the Social-Democratic Fighting Organization posted a proclamation on the walls of Moscow in which it gave the following technical instructions to insurgents:
> 1. The first rule: do not act as a crowd. Act in small groups of three or four, not more. But let the number of such groups be as large as possible and let each of them learn to attack quickly and to disappear as quickly. The police are trying to use units of a hundred cossacks to fire on crowds of several thousands.

14

What you must do is to put one or two marksmen against a hundred cossacks. It is easier to hit a hundred men than a single man, especially if the single man fires without warning and disappears, no one knows where.

2. Also, comrades, do not occupy fortified buildings. The troops will always recapture them or simply destroy them by artillery fire. Let our fortresses be courtyards with entrances front and back, and all places from which it is easy to fire and easy to withdraw. Even if they capture such a place, they will find no one, yet it will cost them dear.[24]

Trotsky quoted these instructions with approval, noting that "the revolutionaries' tactics were promptly determined by the situation itself".[25] These tactics inflicted casualties upon the army while conserving the limited military capability of the revolution. Trotsky realized that this latter consideration was crucial.

How large, in reality were the fighting forces of the insurrection? They were negligible. The party *druzhina* comprised between 700 and 800 men – 500 social democrats and 250 to 300 socialist revolutionaries. Approximately 500 railwaymen equipped with firearms operated at the stations and along the lines. Approximately 400 armed men from among the print-shop operatives and shop assistants made up the auxiliary units. There were also some groups of unattached sharpshooters.[26]

Proper tactics would maximize the destructive potential of this small force, but their real strength sprang from the support of the masses. Trotsky was one of the first to discern this important source of guerrilla vitality which amplified the military impact of a few armed men.

The million-strong population formed a living wall between the guerrillas and the government troops. There were only a few hundred *druzhiniki*. But the barricades were built and rebuilt by the masses. The people surrounded the armed revolutionaries with an atmosphere of active sympathy, foiling the government's plan wherever they could.[27]

In short, "the *druzhina* is almost invulnerable because it is clad in the armor of popular sympathy".[28]

But the miniscule military force available to the revolution was unable to make effective use of the enthusiasm of the masses. It was as if an emaciated pygmy had dressed himself in heavy plate armor.

The strength of the revolutionaries was simply insufficient for them to direct the efforts of the masses. The situation was made even more disastrous by the fact that the tsarist troops were not unwilling to shoot holes in the living armor in order to destroy their opponents. Unless the revolution's army could become much stronger, achieving victory in open battle appeared to be impossible. There was little chance that a powerful force could be developed under conditions of tsarist repression. Thus the attractive hope that the revolution could destroy its foes in pitched battle seemed impractical under the conditions existing in Russia after the failure of 1905. Rather than stake the success of the revolution on the existence of a force that might be impossible to develop, Trotsky investigated the alternative. If the revolutionary masses could win the conflict by dying for their revolutionary ideals there would be no need to await the development of powerful fighting organizations.

THE ROLE OF THE MASSES IN THE FIGHT
AGAINST REPRESSION

There were obvious difficulties inherent in this alternative. It presupposed a dramatic encounter between crowds of workers and tsarist soldiers in which the former would demonstrate enthusiasm for the revolutionary cause by laying down their lives. This would destroy the soldiers' resolve, and the revolutionary victory would be achieved when the soliders threw down their arms and went over to the side of the workers. A moral problem arose from the fact that this might require the death of thousands. Political problems were almost sure to result from the fact that a large percentage of the massive casualty list would be made up of the most politically aware elements of the working class who were willing to take part in demonstrations. Decimation of this group was dangerous since the Social Democrats depended upon it for support. However, these problems might be offset by the fact that the very spontaneity of this approach to revolutionary confrontation made victory possible in spite of tsarist security measures. The repression which prevented the formation of a revolutionary fighting organization might very well foster the discontent which would contribute to success through mass sacrifice.

This practical consideration seems to have prompted Trotsky to contemplate the alternative of dying for the revolution in the defense speech. He stated that "a popular rising has been 'prepared' not when the people have been armed with rifles and guns – for in that case it could never be prepared – but when it is armed with

16

readiness to die in open street battle".[29] He also outlined the actions which had been taken to prepare the masses for this fate.

> To prepare for it [insurrection of the masses] meant, for us, doing everything possible to minimize the casualties of this inevitable conflict. Did we think that for this purpose we had first of all to lay in stocks of arms, prepare a plan of military operations, assign the participants of the rising to particular places, divide the town into sectors — in other words, do all the things which the military authorities do in anticipation of "disorders," when they divide Petersburg up into sectors, appoint colonels in charge of each sector and equip them with a certain number of machine guns and ammunition? No, that is not how we interpreted our role. To prepare for an inevitable insurrection — and, gentlemen of the court, we never *prepared an insurrection* as the prosecution thinks and says; we prepared *for* an insurrection — meant to us, first and foremost, enlightening the people, explaining to them that open conflict was inevitable, that all that had been given to them would be taken away again, that only might can defend right, that the struggle had to be continued to the end, that there was no other way. That is what preparing an insurrection meant to us.[30]

The assertion that the Social Democrats had not been engaged in insurrectionary activity is inexact. Military Committees of the RSDLP had been busy preparing an insurrection as well as preparing for an insurrection, and Trotsky himself had been calling for such action ever since his return from emigration. In his defense Trotsky was attempting to denigrate and perhaps even to deny these unsuccessful efforts at insurrection and turn the court's attention to other actions of the Soviet which, he argued, transcended the narrow limits of tsarist laws designed to cope with revolution. Even though the approach was disingenuous, the argument was sincere, for those attempts to prepare an insurrection were woefully weak and had shown little promise for victory. By the time he made his defense speech Trotsky was willing to develop the notion that dying for the revolution was the necessary alternative because it might never be possible to marshal sufficient forces to gain a conventional victory. He saw revolutionary events moving the masses beyond bourgeois conventionality, and just as this made their representative institutions incomprehensible to non-revolutionary observers, it also transformed their military tactics, committing them irrevocably to mass action, even though the masses were not armed.

The fundamental consideration which led Trotsky to this conclusion is found in this same speech: "Under what conditions did we think an insurrection might lead us to victory? The condition of the army's sympathy."[31] The army must *support* the revolution; it must actively participate on the side of the revolutionaries rather than on the side of the government. This is the essence of successful revolution, but how is it to be achieved? Trotsky discerned two interrelated methods: weaken the army and strengthen the crowd. In this mode of thought Trotsky was not merely thinking of weakening the army in the classical methods of military confrontation. He went beyond consideration of casualties, logistics, troops available, etc. and stressed discipline, morale, and motivation – the factors which determine an army's will to fight. It appeared that this will to fight was the army's vulnerable point against which the real power of the revolution could be brought to bear before the armed clash occurred. Then, when the confrontation with resolute crowds took place, the army would lack resolve and would turn upon its officers, destroying them and assisting in the movement toward revolutionary victory.

Events occurring in 1905 made this approach seem feasible. The first heartening incident was the mutiny of the crew aboard the battleship *Potemkin* of the Black Sea Fleet in mid-June. In October and November serious disturbances and revolts occurred among sailors and soldiers at Kronstadt, Sevastopol, and elsewhere. By that time conditions in some reserve units awaiting return from the Far East had become so serious that the government considered granting them plots of land in the Far East and leaving them there to avoid further contamination of non-mutinous units.[32] It seemed that the army was on the verge of breaking apart, and the revolutionaries took whatever steps they could to accelerate the process.

The proclamation of the St. Petersburg Central Committee of the RSDLP to soldiers and sailors on the occasion of the *Potemkin* mutiny reveals the primary hope of the revolutionaries that the men in the ranks would see their unity with the revolutionary masses:

> Open your eyes and ears. You have been isolated from the people by your officers and priests who would soil your hands with the blood of the workers, who would turn you against women, children, and the aged. A new day has come in Russia. Form Soldiers' Soviets. Recognize your brotherhood with the workers. Soldiers of the Russian army and fleet – a great event has occurred in the Black Sea. The sailors of the *Potemkin* openly and boldly have come to side with the workers. They have torn down the Tsarist flag which represents slavery and

18

repression and raised the red flag signifying freedom and brotherhood .... Follow the example of the *Potemkin* — seize power; come to the side of the workers. If your officers stand in your way they should be the first to die in the battle for justice, freedom, and for the people.[33]

Establishment of this unity between revolutionary and soldier would assure victory, since it would be impossible for the military officers to assert their authority once this condition had been established. However, even though this goal had been clearly articulated in June, and in spite of the fact that the discipline and resolve of the army was eroding, the goal was not achieved, and in its last days the Soviet was still issuing hopeful manifestos:

> Your troubles are our troubles, your needs our needs, your struggle our struggle. Our victory will be your victory. We are bound by the same chains. Only the united efforts of the people and the army will break those chains.[34]

In retrospect Trotsky concluded that unity could not be established because the proletarian leaven within the army was simply inadequate for the task. Far too many soldiers were unenlightened peasants who were unaccustomed to challenging authority, were totally lacking in political consciousness, and thus were beyond the reach of revolutionary propaganda.[35]

As a result of this weakness of the proletarian element within the army, military units did not respond to the situation in 1905 as the authors of the unity manifestos had hoped they would. In fact, the military units which mutinied found that they had to overcome powerful reactionary forces within their own ranks before they could be of any real use to the revolution. Most mutinous units never succeeded in this task; however, the nature of their struggle seemed to confirm the earlier assessments of Marx and Engels that mass conscription would weaken the modern army's ability to suppress revolution. It appeared that these struggles within army units reflected the class composition of the units. This notion was stated explicitly by Trotsky.

> Friction between the proletarian minority and the peasant majority in the armed forces is a characteristic of all our military risings, and it paralyzes them and robs them of power. The workers carry their class advantages with them to the barracks: intelligence, technical training, resoluteness, and ability for concerted action. The peasants contribute their overwhelming numerical strength. The army, by universal

19

conscription, overcomes the muzhik's lack of productive coordination in a mechanical way, and his passivity, his chief political fault, is transformed into an irreplaceable virtue. Even when the peasant regiments are drawn into the revolutionary movement on the ground of their immediate needs, they are always inclined to adopt wait and see tactics, and at the enemy's first decisive attack they abandon the "mutineers" and allow themselves to be placed once more under the disciplinary yoke.[36]

Trotsky went beyond these generalizations in his analysis of the Sevastopol uprising where he noted that

it was the sappers who were most resolute in joining the sailors; they came armed, and took up quarters in the naval barracks. The same fact can be observed in all revolutionary movements in our army: the most revolutionary are sappers, engineers, gunners, in short, not the gray illiterates of the infantry, but skilled, highly literate technically trained soliders. To this difference at the intellectual level corresponds one of social origin: the vast majority of infantry soldiers are young peasants, whereas the engineers and gunners are recruited chiefly from among industrial workers.[37]

The same considerations of literacy and familiarity with machines which led to a concentration of factory workers in the artilllery and the engineers also contributed to the great number of urban draftees in the navy. Sophisticated mechanics were needed to maintain and operate the engine rooms of the modern steam-powered naval vessels, and their breech-loaded rifled guns required highly trained crews. In Trotsky's opinion these class considerations which made the navy a potential hotbed of revolutionary activity were further enhanced by other factors. In discussing the Black Sea Mutiny he noted:

The very nature of their activity demands from sailors a greater degree of independence and resourcefulness, makes them more self-reliant than land soliders. The antagonism between common sailors and the closed upperclass caste of naval officers is even deeper than it is in the army, where half of the officers are plebians. Lastly, the disgrace of the Russo-Japanese War, the onus of which had been borne by the navy, destroyed any last vestiges of respect the sailors might still have had for their grasping and cowardly captains and admirals.[38]

But in spite of this potential for vital revolutionary activity, the military initiated few victories for the revolutionary cause in 1905, and, as Trotsky seemed to realize, the lack of any really dynamic revolutionary initiative within the military put the revolutionary leadership in an extremely difficult position. Lacking an uprising within the military which could serve as a revolutionary catalyst, the revolutionary leaders had to give their support to the dangerously weak revolutionary elements within the military in the hope that this support might be sufficient to allow embryonic military-revolutionary movements to gain control of military units. These units could then be used to defend and expand the revolution. This was the hope which motivated the St. Petersburg Soviet of Workers' Deputies when they supported the Kronstadt Mutiny.

The soldiers and sailors at the Kronstadt Naval Base and Fortress, being in close geographic proximity to the revolutionary activity of October in St. Petersburg, had enjoyed greater freedom and were quite naturally excited by the October Manifesto. They were unenthusiastic about returning to the strict discipline of earlier times, even though their officers attempted to restore it. Incidence of disobedience rose, and a number of soldiers were imprisoned to await trial for insubordination. On 26 October a group of sailors attempted to free them by force of arms, and a general mutiny ensued. The mutineers broke into the main arsenal, and, having armed thelselves, roamed the fortress and town of Kronstadt.[39] The St. Petersburg Soviet saw the mutiny as an opportunity for a mass demonstration of solidarity between workers and soldiers which could neutralize the local armed forces as a counter-revolutionary force. In retrospect, Trotsky interpreted this as a critical moment in the development of the Soviet's power.

> The Soviet was increasingly concerned with extending its influence over the army and the peasantry. In November the Soviet called upon the workers to express actively their fraternal solidarity with the awakening army as personified by the Kronstadt sailors. Not to do this would have been to refuse to extend the Soviet's strength. To do it was a step towards the coming conflict.[40]

The Soviet called upon the workers of St. Petersburg to go out on strike in sympathy for the Kronstadters. Having taken this action without plans and with no real forces at its disposal, the St. Petersburg Soviet was embarking on a course of action that required complete faith in mass confrontation as a means of eroding the resolve of the military forces of repression to guarantee the victory of the revolution. Trotsky argued that the selection of this course of action was unavoidable and that it had some chance of producing the expected victory.

In Trotsky's interpretation of events, mass action initiated by the Soviet became inevitable after Witte rejected the 18 October Soviet proposal for the withdrawal of troops from the capital.[41]

> What was the Soviet to do? Either it had to withdraw, leaving the matter in the hands of the chamber of conciliation, the future State Duma, which is what the liberals really wanted; or it had to prepare to hold on with armed power to everything that had been won in October, and, if possible, to launch a further offensive.[42]

Obviously the first alternative did not appeal to the leader of the Soviet, and the second alternative could not take place under better conditions than those offered by the Kronstadt uprising. But the expected results were not achieved. Even though about one hundred and twenty thousand St. Petersburg workers went out on strike to show their sympathy for the Kronstadt sailors, a direct confrontation between the striking masses and the army did not develop.[43] The government had begun to learn some more sophisticated techniques for dealing with mass actions, and it made minor concessions (agreeing to try the 3,000 mutineers at regular courts martial rather than at field courts martial) which reduced the political effectiveness of the strike. The bloodbath which would have horrified the demoralized military units and brought their revolutionary elements to ascendency never occurred, and Trotsky was left to speculate on what its results might have been.

He was convinced that successful revolution would have followed.

> In struggle it is extremely important to weaken the enemy. That is what a strike does. At the same time a strike brings the army of the revolution to its feet. But neither one nor the other, in itself, creates a state revolution. The power still has to be snatched from the hands of the old rulers and handed over to the revolution. That is the fundamental task. A general strike only creates the necessary preconditions; it is quite inadequate for achieving the task itself.
>
> The old state power rests on its material forces and, above all, on the army. The army stands in the way of real, as opposed to paper, revolution. At a certain moment in revolution the crucial question becomes: on which side are the soldiers – their sympathies and their bayonets? That is not a question you can answer with the help of a questionnaire. Many useful and appropriate comments can be made concerning the width and

straightness of streets in modern towns, the characteristics of modern weapons, etc., etc., but none of these technical considerations can supersede the question of the revolutionary takeover of state power. The inertia of the army must be overcome. The revolution achieves this by pitting the army against the popular masses. A general strike creates favorable conditions for such conflict. It is a harsh method, but history offers no other.[44]

Circumstances had not provided this opportunity to the St. Petersburg revolutionaries, for the direct interaction between the striking workers and the government's forces of repression did not occur. As we have already seen, when the clash finally came in Moscow in December, it did not take the form that Trotsky had hoped it would. Once again it proved impossible to bring the masses into direct conflict with the armed forces, and the ensuing guerrilla warfare proved to be inadequate to the revolution's needs.

OTHER FACTORS CONTRIBUTING TO VICTORY IN THE REVOLUTION

The inadequacy of the military programs of the revolution led Trotsky to give some rather careful thought to some of the other causal factors which might have explained the defeat of the revolution. He was aware that timing is extremely important in military endeavors, and he considered the possibility that more appropriate moments for action might have been chosen. Perhaps the revolution dissipated its forces when it should have been husbanding them. However, we must recall that Trotsky considered conflict inevitable and he saw the conflict itself as having beneficial effects. Since one of the obstacles that the revolution had to overcome was "the inertia of the military", revolutionary challenge was essential for the polarization process which would bring revolutionary success. Therefore, avoiding battle because of conventional "balance of forces" considerations was not necessarily wise. Trotsky also knew that the revolutionary leadership was dependent upon the mood of the revolutionary masses. This mood was not a function of the correlation of military forces but was instead a manifestation of basic economic and political realities which drove the masses to direct action. When direct action led to confrontation with military units conventional military considerations governing the decision to give or to avoid battle (comparative strength, armament, and disposition of forces as well as tactical or logistical advantages) could not be applied. In addition, the confrontation or individual battle had to be viewed not in terms of its outcome as a discrete event but rather in terms of the revolutionary campaign.

> In revolution, even more than in war, the moment of battle is determined less by calculation on either side than by the respective position of both the opposition armies. It is true that in war, owing to the mechanical discipline of armies, it is sometimes possible to lead an entire army away from the field of battle without any engagement taking place; yet in such cases the military commander must still ask himself whether the strategy of retreat will not demoralize his troops and whether, by avoiding today's battle, he is not preparing the ground for a more disastrous one tomorrow. General Kuropatkin might have a great deal to say on that point. But in a developing revolutionary situation a planned retreat is, from the start, unthinkable. A party may have the masses behind it while it is attacking, but that does not mean that it will be able to lead them away at will in the midst of the attack. It is not only the party that leads the masses; the masses, in turn, sweep the party forward.[45]

Having thus rejected the possibility that the timing of confrontation could be determined by the revolutionary leadership, and having become convinced that this confrontation was the critical factor in the transfer of power into the hands of the revolution, Trotsky had put himself in a position that made formulation of revolutionary military theory very difficult. Conflict must occur, yet how could the chances of a successful outcome be maximized? This is the question that all military theory seeks to answer, but Trotsky's analysis of the military situation of the revolution offered no definitive answers. The notion that the revolution could fight the government into submission through conventional or guerrilla warfare did not seem tenable, and the notion that the revolutionary masses could establish their solidarity with the misguided elements in a modern mass army through bloody sacrifice did not seem manageable. In what appears to have been a rather half-hearted attempt to overcome this difficulty, Trotsky tried to link the two approaches into a chronological relationship with the guerrilla phase leading into the mass confrontation:

> an insurrection is, in essence, not so much a struggle against the army as a struggle *for* the army. The more stubborn, far-reaching, and successful the insurrection, the more probable –

indeed inevitable – is a fundamental change in the attitude of the troops. Guerrilla fighting on the basis of a revolutionary strike cannot in itself, as we saw in Moscow, lead to victory. But it creates the possibility of sounding the mood of the army, and after a first important victory – that is, once part of the garrison has joined the insurrection – the guerrilla struggle can be transformed into a mass struggle in which a part of the troops, supported by the armed and unarmed population, will fight another part, which will find itself in a ring of universal hatred.[46]

But this approach has obvious flaws. The most critical is the possibility that politically neutral military units will be polarized *against* the revolution by guerrilla tactics. Taking casualties changes the psychological composition of a military unit. It becomes enemy-oriented: suspicious of outsiders, proud of the risks it is taking, and full of hate for those who inflict the casualties. In such a situation the traditional rank structure can work effectively to maintain the upper hand, easily convincing the non-aligned elements within the unit that a virulent force is operating in society which must be destroyed before it can destroy the soldiers themselves. Units thrown into this survival mode of thinking can easily develop a solid counter-revolutionary front, perceiving the revolutionary guerrillas as cowardly killers who hide behind the people and refuse open battle. Once this state of consciousness is reached the unit is capable of creating the sort of bloodbath Trotsky thought would be decisive, but while piling up the corpses, the soldiers can still feel as if they are defending themselves. Thus guerrilla tactics may not lead to mass confrontation and revolutionary victory. These tactics may instead engender conditions which make the prospect of successfully revo-lutionizing the army extremely doubtful.[47]

The confusion and contradictions which we have encountered in Trotsky's military thought after 1905 highlight the tentative nature of his theories. He saw merit in both guerrilla warfare and mass confrontation, yet had no clear ideas to explain how the first phase could be transformed into the second. He had only the most primitive knowledge of factors which determined soldiers' individual or collective actions in revolutionary situations. He seemed to have no appreciation for the difficulties encountered in attempting to develop a revolutionary consciousness in the ranks of the military. The army was viewed as a critical yet almost monolithic element in the revolutionary struggle which could be seized like a barricade, not being transformed by the struggle. Later experiences would temper this judgment, but before moving on to later developments it is necessary to investigate the political controversy within the Russian revolutionary left which seems to have played such an important part in retarding the development of Trotsky's military thinking in this period.

CHAPTER THREE

The Russian Social Democrats and Military–Revolutionary Activity, 1905–1912

If failure in revolution does not destroy the revolutionary theoreticians, a valuable opportunity for retrospective criticism and analysis has been attained. This was Trotsky's situation when he wrote *1905*. Defeated in revolution, tried, found guilty, and exiled to Siberia, he made a dramatic escape to émigré life early in 1907.[1] By that time reaction had engulfed Russia. Russian revolutionaries who survived in emigration were forced to analyse the causes of defeat, and in this questioning atmosphere Trotsky wrote his analysis of the experiences of 1905, publishing the first edition in 1908. We have already seen that he brought forth few clear answers for the military problems unsolved in 1905, but how should this shortcoming be explained? The simplest answer is that Trotsky lacked experience, had given little thought to military questions before 1905, and was therefore incapable of rendering sophisticated judgments on military matters.[2] Of course this is true, but such an interpretation fails to take cognizance of the larger questions which structured Trotsky's thinking during this period.

DISAGREEMENTS OVER THE ROLE OF VIOLENCE

The most important of these questions was the reunification of the Russian Marxist factions. If the factions could be brought together the possibility of successful revolution would be greatly enhanced, and Trotsky set himself the task of being an active agent of the unification. Settling in Vienna, Trotsky began to bring his talents to bear on the problems of reducing the differences between the Bolshevik and Menshevik factions of the Russian Social Democratic Labor Party (RSDLP).[3] It is in the light of this role of self-styled mediator operating in an atmosphere of introspective criticism of recent failures that Trotsky's analysis of the military lessons of 1905 should be viewed. When this is done, we discover that much of his ambivalence is not the product of ignorance or inexperience but

27

instead reflects an attempt to reconcile the points of view taken by the Mensheviks and Bolsheviks in their study of the military lessons of 1905.

The relationship between revolutionary violence and revolutionary victory was a critical problem facing the Russian Marxists in the early twentieth century. Socialist Revolutionary (SR) groups argued the efficacy of terror, believing that it would galvanize the masses and engender revolutionary action. Generally speaking, the Russian Social Democrats (SDs) rejected this notion, sharing the view expressed by Plekhanov in 1902 that "the idea that terrorism can inspire a mass uprising is wrong".[4] However, there were factions such as the "Volia" group of Social Democrats who sought unity between Russian SDs and SRs, and the SD rejection of terrorism had never really been complete.[5]

The SR proposals for the use of revolutionary violence had been strongly condemned by Plekhanov long before the revolution of 1905. In December 1901 he had written that "the terrorists waste all their efforts on their acts and thus establish no links with the masses".[6] This approach was to be avoided by the Social Democrats, who

> must work through the masses. Their party will still be small, like the staff of an army, but it will be directly engaged in guiding the revolutionary efforts of the masses. Terrorists think only in terms of examples, without understanding the masses.[7]

Later, in conjunction with May Day activities in 1902, Plekhanov had rejected the terrorists' faith in assassination as a means of engendering revolution. In discussing a recent Socialist Revolutionary brochure, "On Street Disorders", Plekhanov noted that the author

> advises that at the very first moment of the conflict between the people and the armed forces, the government's political and military leadership must be immediately "taken out of circulation". This advice, in and of itself, is really very good. The revolutionary Social Democrats probably would agree with the author in taking this step, but only after they have gained the position of leadership in the minds of the masses engaged in revolutionary activity. Then it would be proper to take the responsibility for an armed uprising having as its objective the destruction of the leadership of the repressive government. That is the proper time – not at the moment when revolutionary activity begins.[8]

In Plekhanov's view violence could not be used to generate revolutionary momentum. In addition, he felt that it could not be organized in advance by the revolutionary leadership through the use of devices such as revolutionary fighting organizations. Continuing his attack on the same pamphlet, Plekhanov wrote:

> The SR writer has proposed the formation of military "dozens" (*desiatka*) which will become close knit units that can be in the forefront of the stuggle with the army and the police. He also postulates that their existence will encourage soldiers to abandon the army and come over to the revolution. But revolution is not made by "details". The significant portion of the masses will be organized not into such "dozens" but in some other fashion. Among the masses there may possibly appear some sort of armed units of workers and students. It is quite possible that these armed *druzhinii* will enhance the progress of the revolution. But we simply cannot predict or prepare the form that the revolution's organization will take at the time of the demonstration. When we organize it, the policeman's fist and the cossack's whip will "make merry on the backs of students, workers, and outside agitators".[9]

The events of 1905 convinced Plekhanov that he had been right when he argued in this fashion, for the outcome of the December Uprising seemed to fulfill the dark predictions found in passages such as the one just cited. Plekhanov opposed the Moscow uprising, and its failure confirmed his belief that "in countries with constitutions workers can march, but not in Russia".[10] He continued to work for the successful bourgeois revolution while discounting the effectiveness of planning the use of revolutionary force.[11]

Plekhanov's leadership continued to attract many Russian Marxists after 1905, and Trotsky seems to have been responding to their point of view when discussing the mass action "dying for the revolution" approach to revolutionary victory. Plekhanov had admitted that the sacrifice of the workers would have a positive effect in gaining support for the revolution, and his belief in the power of the masses was unshaken.[12] When Trotsky was writing about confrontation between great masses of revolutionaries and irresolute army units, he was working out the revolutionary scenario acceptable to this group, and his ultimate acceptance of this type of confrontation as the decisive point in the movement toward revolutionary victory can be seen as an indication of his sympathy for the ideological position which insisted on mass action as the real key to success.

However, after 1905 there were numerous Russian Marxists who rejected Plekhanov's approach. Lenin's Bolsheviks were thinking in terms of an armed clash, and they were preparing to work directly upon the army to enhance the chances for success. During 1905 Lenin had become convinced that the revolution was arming itself in preparation for an open conflict with the army. Shortly after the *Potemkin* uprising he had written of the apparent revolutionary progression: "Riots – demonstrations – street disorders – detachments of a revolutionary army – through such stages the popular uprising is developed".[13] At the same time he had commented on the conflict between forces of revolution and reaction:

> The armed struggle between the workers and the tsarist forces has begun. The street fighting and the battle at the barricades has begun. Events in the Caucasus, in Lodz', and in Odessa have convinced us of the heroism and enthusiasm of the proletariat. The struggle has been transformed into an uprising.... The army is beginning to waver. There are isolated instances of insubordination, outbursts among the reserves, protests by officers, agitation among soldiers, refusals of separate companies or regiments to fire on their brother workers. *Thus elements of the army come over to the side of the revolution.* The greatest significance of the recent events in Odessa lies in the fact that this is the first time that a major unit of tsarist military force – an entire battleship – has openly come over to the side of the revolution.[14]

The struggle was to be openly fought, and its outcome would be determined by the vitality of the revolutionary movement within the army, for the units that passed over to the side of the revolutionaries would form "the nucleus of the revolutionary army" which could be used to ensure victory over the military detachments that had refused to join the revolution.[15]

When the Moscow Uprising occurred in December, Lenin continued to embrace these notions. In this article, "On the Lessons of the Moscow Uprising", published in August 1906, he directly attacked Plekhanov's assertion that the workers erred in arming themselves and seeking to give battle from barricades.[16] Lenin pointed out that revolutionary enthusiasm should not be constrained and that the fight at the barricades was really a "struggle for the army", which could only have a successful outcome if the army was met on its own terms (by force).[17] In addition, the events in Moscow had convinced Lenin that the revolution would need trained military leaders who could organize the patrolling and defending of the barricaded areas while training the workers in the use of the modern sophisticated weapons which might be captured in battle.[18] But most important, Lenin now became an advocate of guerrilla warfare. Following Engels' lead in believing that military tactics were a function of military technology, Lenin wrote:

> Military technology today is not the same as that of the latter half of the nineteenth century. To deploy great flocks of people and to defend barricades with revolvers when confronted by artillery would be sheer folly. So Kautsky was right when he wrote that after Moscow the time has come to use Engels to derive "new tactics for the barricades". These tactics are those of partisan warfare. The organizations which evolved because of the necessity to employ such tactics were highly mobile and extremely small detachments of ten, three, or perhaps even only two men. One often encounters Social Democrats who titter when the discussion turns to the actions of a few men, but such tittering is only a girlish way of hiding eyes that are closed to the new problems of tactics and organization.[19]

Lenin's writings immediately after the 1905 revolution thus made it perfectly clear that he had accepted the approach of "fighting for the revolution" with armed guerrillas which Trotsky wrote about a year later in his analysis of 1905. The line between Plekhanov and Lenin was clearly drawn on the question of military tactics in the revolutionary situation. Trotsky sided with neither. His analysis of the two alternatives in *1905* found advantages and disadvantages in each. He saw conflict with the army as inevitable, but neither Plekhanov's nor Lenin's approach guaranteed success in future confrontations.

MILITARY–REVOLUTIONARY THEORY AND PARTY ORGANIZATION

The delineation between Bolshevik and Menshevik views concerning military revolutionary tactics can be traced all the way back to Lenin's call for military organizations to carry out party work of agitation and propaganda in army units, which had appeared in "What is to be Done?" in 1902.[20] However, the differences on questions of military-revolutionary theory were obscured by the larger questions of party organization and party attitudes toward bougeois liberalism. It was the post-October events of the 1905 revolution which caused the difference of opinion to surface. Military-revolutionary theory then became a major issue in the debates which raged between the Fourth (Unity) Party Congress of the RSDLP (held in Stockholm in late April, 1906) and the Fifth Party Congress (held in London in May, 1907). After the Fifth Party Congress the Bolshevik–Menshevik split seemed permanent to both sides, and the debate subsided, leaving the field open for men such as Trotsky who were trying to tread the middle ground and bring the two factions back together. In this attempt Trotsky drew heavily upon the alternatives posited by the two factions in the earlier debates, and therefore an understanding of those arguments is essential to an appreciation of the origins of Trotsky's writings on the military lessons of 1905.

The fundamental differences between the Bolshevik and Menshevik factions on the military-revolutionary question had emerged on two issues debated at the Fourth Party Congress. The first of these was the role of the armed uprising (*vooruzhennoe vosstanie*), and the second was the significance of partisan uprisings, or partisan militant uprisings (*partizanskie boevye vystuplenniia*) as they were called by the Bolsheviks. In both cases, the Congress ultimately rejected the Bolshevik proposals, but Lenin characteristically continued to insist on the correctness of the Bolshevik position.

In their proposed resolution on armed uprising the Bolsheviks presented the view that the events of 1905, with their partial victories for the working class, had established the pre-conditions for a chain of events in which armed uprising would be of central importance.[21] This argument was predicated upon several observations. First, the Bolsheviks felt that there were forces at work which would broaden the democratic revolution in Russia, turning it into a mass movement which would encompass the entire country and lead to a decisive offensive struggle against the autocracy. They also felt that the October strike reflected the vitality of the strength of the Russian proletariat and justified continued optimism on the part of Russian Marxists, since the strike had failed not because of the weakness of the masses but because of the weakness of the class organizations which should have guided the masses. However, they also argued that the continuation of strike tactics after October dissipated the revolutionary strength of the masses.[22] The second major point in their argument was that the Moscow Uprising in December was the next logical step in the revolutionary experience, having resulted from the elemental strength inherent in the mass movement being frustrated in the attempt to continue using peaceful strikes and demonstrations to attain the goals of the revolution. The December Uprising was seen as a further widening of the revolution since it led to the arming of the urban poor and the peasants who then were forced to defend the people's gains against the armed force of the government. In addition, the Bolsheviks felt that the December Uprising transformed as well as widened the revolution, in that it brought forth new tactics for fighting behind barricades and demonstrated the feasibility of armed workers engaging in open conflict with a modern army. Finally, the Bolsheviks argued that the entire revolutionary experience of 1905, with its tastes of victory followed by the bitter fruits of defeat, had convinced the workers that they could not trust the promises of the government and had led them to realize that they could only gain real power after a victorious open struggle with the forces of autocracy. At the same time the 1905 revolution had made that victory easier to win by weakening and demoralizing the armed forces. The revolution had forced the autocracy to use the army to suppress the population, an act which in itself had weakened the army, but which would have even greater long term repercussions in that it had prevented the implementation of badly-needed reforms within the army itself. In the absence of these reforms the army would be easily defeated in a future conflict with the masses.

The Bolshevik resolutions which were based upon these considerations followed logically from this interpretation of 1905, but they were a radical departure from classical Marxian theory. The Bolsheviks proposed that the Congress resolve that armed uprising was a desirable and necessary step in the successful revolution, and that its importance was greater than that of the general strike. The armed uprising would be decisive, and therefore all other considerations, such as the time and place of strikes as well as the Party resources to be expended on such secondary activities, would be subordinated to the necessities of the armed uprising.

Since the armed uprising would be the main form of struggle, the Bolsheviks expected the Congress to resolve that the Party would give great emphasis to studying the practical lessons of the December Uprising so that a systematic military critique of its strengths and weaknesses could be extracted. This set of lessons could then be used to develop a doctrine of insurgency which could be used as a guide in the future.

Greater emphasis also was called for in the recruiting, training, and arming of military bands so that the Party could have a fighting arm prepared to assume the leadership in future uprisings. The Bolsheviks also called for a resolution that would take cognizance of the need for this military leadership. They admitted that a successful uprising could occur only if there was a background of discontent, but they wanted the Congress to resolve that this discontent had to be reinforced by the presence of an organized leadership having the goal of decisive confrontation with the government. Almost all of these proposed resolutions would shock the Mensheviks a bit, but the Bolsheviks had saved the most upsetting proposal to conclude their proposal on armed uprising.

> We acknowledge and propose for the congress to approve ... that with the introduction of a growing peasant movement which may blow up rapidly into a full-scale uprising at any time in the future, it is desirable to take steps to strengthen the union for action between peasants and workers with an organization enhancing a united and simultaneous military insurrection.[23]

This statement of the need to develop an alliance with the countryside was clearly contrary to the Menshevik position on revolutionary action, and it could only serve to exacerbate the differences between the factions. This was exactly what happened. In the end, many of the Bolshevik proposals were defeated, but the resolution finally adopted still retained some elements of the Bolshevik program, and surprisingly, these included watered-down statements of the importance of the peasantry.

The resolution on armed uprising adopted by the Fourth Party Congress was much more cautious in its approach than that proposed by the Bolsheviks.[24] It rejected the call for the formation of armed bands to lead the proletariat into battle, and it played down the importance of an open armed clash between workers and soldiers. The Congress was willing to accept the Bolshevik assertion that an armed uprising was necessary to seize power from the ruling elite, but the nature of the conflict was perceived differently. The Congress agreed with the Bolshevik assessment that the army had been weakened by the government's failure to implement reforms within the military, but it accepted the Menshevik interpretation of the significance of this fact.

According to this interpretation the result of the weakening of the army which would enhance the chances for revolutionary success was to be the defection of large parts of the army to the side of the workers. The resolution proclaimed that victory was inconceivable unless this occurred. The resolution also reflected the Menshevik belief that success in the armed uprising could be assured only if the uprising was a mass action resulting from extreme social and economic tensions. Militant actions by small groups or individuals could not enhance the progress of the revolution. Based upon these considerations, the Congress passed several specific resolutions on armed uprising.

The first of these stated that the fundamental task of the party was the development of revolutionary potential through broad-based agitational activities among the proletariat, peasantry, urban petty bourgeoisie, and troops. These activities would be designed to maximize the growth of the Party while helping the people to understand the impossibility of a fundamental agreement with the tsarist government and the inevitability of the need to use the armed force to realize the revolution's political expectations. These activites were to be primarily open (legal), so that they would establish the appeal of the Social Democratic program while reinforcing the legitimacy of SD leadership.

The second specific resolution rejected the Bolshevik notion that the Party should attempt to arm the workers. Recognizing that sufficient resources for such a task simply were not available, the Party proclaimed that it could not take the responsibility for arousing false hopes in the prospect of an armed population and would have to restrict its goals to promoting self-arming of the population while organizing and arming military bands which would be capable of planning the insurrectionary struggle and taking the initiative at the proper moment. However, the third resolution indicated that these armed bands were to be cautious in the exercise of the initiative, for its plainly stated the Party would leave to its opposition all attempts to draw the proletariat into an armed clash under unfavourable conditions. Destroying the gains made through agitation by leading a premature insurrection and thus discrediting the Party's ability to discern the proper course of action was to be avoided wherever possible.

The final resolution allowed Party committees to work with groups from these other oppositional parties to coordinate the actions of participants in armed uprisings, but it stressed the fact that this work would be of secondary importance. Party committees designated to prepare the uprising would concentrate primarily upon organizing and propagandizing within the army and within military educational institutions, and in all of their activities they would subordinate themselves to the will of the Central Committee of the Party. The Central Committee would assume responsibility for determining the critical lessons which were to be drawn from the experiences of 1905 and would pass these to the local military organizations for implementation.

The provisions of the Party resolution were politically sound in that they would save the Party from being identified with an unsuccessful cause. However, the costs in terms of military preparedness were significant. By allowing other party groups (presumably the terrorist elements of the SRs) to assume the leadership in military revolutionary activity, the Social Democrats emasculated their own military organizations.

In the context of the repressive tsarist police system, preparation for military revolutionary leadership implied a number of specific actions. The party which accepted this responsibility would develop a cadre of military leaders even though the possibility of infiltration made this a risky course of action. It would procure and maintain caches of small arms, ammunition, and bombs to be used in initial battles with the armed forces in spite of the fact that discovery of these materials by the secret police would lead to immediate prosecution. It would train workers in weaponry and tactics so that effective action would be possible when an opportunity arose even though these attempts to prepare for insurrection multiplied the chances of arrest.

All of these actions were risky, but the party which was even partially successful in carrying them out would enjoy great advantages when an insurrection occurred. Its leadership would be highly visible in the confrontation with the military, and the expertise this leadership could display would make its contributions seem invaluable to the crowd. At the same time, its ability to provide weapons as well as leadership would further enhance its stature. None of these things could be done by a party which had not planned and labored to prepare for assuming military leadership when the opportunity arose. Therefore, avoiding responsibility because the result of the uprising might be unfavourable had serious implications.

The Party resolution and the Bolshevik proposal which preceded it illustrate divergent theories on the nature of the Party's role in preparing armed uprising and the nature of the uprising itself. The Bolsheviks were thinking almost exclusively in terms of the development of fighting resources to bring victory in open battle while the Menshevik faction was hoping that mass action would undermine the military, weaken its resolve, and make the confrontation between the masses and the army as bloodless as possible. Yet on this question agreement seemed to have outweighed disagreement, and most of Lenin's conditions could be met in the final resolution on the armed uprising. Both sides agreed that such a clash was inevitable, and the details were not impossible to agree upon once this substantial point of commonality had been recognized. The Congress's consideration of the question of partisan warfare did not result in an equally happy solution. The Bolsheviks and Mensheviks did not share common viewpoints on this issue, and the results reflect the fundamental conflict.

The Bolsheviks had come to the Congress with a prepared

resolution on the subject of partisan militant uprisings.[25] Their draft observed that armed conflict between rebellious forces and the military was still endemic in Russia, with the revolutionary elements having resorted to partisan warfare as a means of carrying on their resistance in spite of growing government repression. This continued conflict was seen as unavoidable, given the fact that there were two hostile forces present in Russia, both of which were armed and bent upon inflicting maximum casualties upon the other. The continued resistance of the partisan elements was seen in a sympathetic light since there seemed to be no alternative to answering violence with violence once the government had embarked on its "debauchery of military repression".

However, the Bolsheviks noted that this continual conflict, although a reflection of the bravery of the partisan fighters, might very well contribute to the disorganization of the forces of revolution and could even retard the preparation for the future open armed conflict between the revolutionary masses and the government forces which would be the decisive point in the course of revolutionary events. While this was a disturbing possibility, there seemed to be no way to control the partisan actions, so the Bolsheviks advocated the use of these conflicts as a means of educating and training the Party's fighting bands. Since these were just beginning to be organized, and since the Bolsheviks felt that fighting organizations had displayed a low level of practical skills in the December Uprising, the opportunity to gain experience was seen as being extremely valuable in the development of the genuine expertise which would be so badly needed if the armed uprising were to follow the Bolshevik scenario with its dependence upon the leadership of specially trained and equipped Party activists.[26]

Based upon these considerations the Bolsheviks resolved that the Party should recognize and support the partisan fighting bands because of the benefits which would accrue from such a policy. Experienced cadres could be attracted into the Party, and methods of offensive and surprise ambush tactics could be studied and practiced. The Party would gain popular acclaim for its part in helping the people resist the outrages of the Black Hundred activists who were using violent methods to bully the population into submission. Finally, the support of partisan activity would allow the Party to become involved in armed actions designed to seize money and arms illegally held by agents of the autocratic government. These could then be used to support wider partisan activities and other party programs designed to speed the coming of the revolution.

This last consideration is of course a part of the Bolsheviks position on expropriation which shocked the Mensheviks just as deeply as it shocked more conservative critics. There were certain problems of principle in the Bolshevik position, in that the actions they were advocating were clearly illegal. But to their critics within the Party the most sensitive problem was a practical one – how was a revolutionary partisan to be distinguished from a bandit? The Bolsheviks were arguing that the distinction was a simple matter: if the partisan organization was willing to accept party discipline and direct its activities towards the achievement of party goals it was truly revolutionary. If it did not accept party discipline, revolutionaries could not judge the legality of its actions by bourgeois standards, but only in terms of whether or not the actions of a given band advanced or retarded the revolutionary cause. Only in the latter case could the group be considered undesirable.

This viewpoint was anathema to the Mensheviks, who were striving to expand the scope of legal Party activities as they sought increased areas of cooperation with the liberals. As a result, while the Mensheviks were willing to grant that repressive actions taken by the government had led to widespread violence, they were unwilling to accept the Bolshevik views concerning the proper relationship between the Party and violent lawless elements.[27] The final resolution on the partisan question, which represented Menshevik views on the subject, therefore rejected much of the "insurgency" theory which was so appealing to the Bolsheviks.[28]

The Party's resolution began with an extremely strong denunciation of tsarist methods which apparently was designed in part to assuage the Bolsheviks. The punitive expeditions, mass executions, and general terroristic tactics of the government were condemned, and the official support of Black Hundreds and the ensuing ethnic hostilities were singled out for special censure. However, this criticism of tsarist policy was followed by the observation

> that the declassed strata of society – criminal offenders and the dregs of the urban population – always take advantage of revolutionary disturbances to pursue their own antisocial goals, and that the revolutionary masses must take severe measures against bacchanalian filching and robbery; and finally that the major force of the revolution is the product of its moral-political influence over the revolutionary masses, the society, and the army, and that with the disorganization of governmental power, the revolution solves its problems through the organization of social forces, not through anarchism.[29]

Having made this rather strong statement against revolutionary opportunism, the Menshevik-inspired resolution specifically called for a struggle "against the actions of individuals or groups seeking to steal money while using the name or motto of the S.D. Party",[30] a measure which directly opposed the Leninist belief in expropriation. Toleration of the seizure of arms and other military equipment was the only exception to this anti-expropriation stance. Capital of the State Bank and of other governmental agencies was defined as property of the people which could not be confiscated or spent without complete public responsibility. Demolishing or damaging public or private buildings and other structures such as bridges and roads was also forbidden, and this measure, together with cautions against threatening the personal safety of private citizens, effectively put the Party on record as being against the bomb-tossing terrorism which the Mensheviks were so anxious to disavow.

The combined effect of the two resolutions on armed uprisings and partisan warfare was frustrating for those Social Democrats who felt that organized fighting for the revolution was the proper course to victory. Fighting organizations were authorized, but the partisan struggles which would develop their skills were forbidden. Lessons of 1905 could be studied, but the conclusions drawn from analysis of those experiences could not be tested. The fighting organizations would be forced to sit idle, waiting for the mass uprising that might never come unless they were allowed to provide the spark that would rouse the masses.

That the situation was unpalatable to the militant members of the Party is understandable. If they were to wait for a spontaneous workers' insurrection before acting they never would be able to act. Unless they had an opportunity to organize and plan for armed confrontation they would not have the resources necessary to channel the efforts of the crowd if an insurrection should develop. The Party would be impotent, and without the leadership of a prepared Party organization the mass movement was foredoomed. The defeat suffered in Moscow would be repeated as long as the Party failed to prepare for the assumption of military leadership.

The political arguments against militants who expressed this view were powerful, though, for it was quite easy to label the militant program as Blanquism. This implied that the tactics to be used relied upon the actions of a secret, strongly organized and centralized, armed organization to begin the revolution by seizing power at the right moment. In Blanquist theory the proletariat would then be drawn into action to support the revolutionary initiative. Blanqui's theories, which failed to take cognizance of the key role to be played

39

by the proletariat, were unacceptable to both factions in the RSDLP. However, Lenin and the other militant SDs accepted the need to organize and prepare the revolution even though they emphasized the necessity for the economic and social preconditions for insurrection which would lead to a powerful revolutionary upsurge within the proletariat. While they argued that revolutionary victory was inconceivable without this upsurge, the similarities between their program and Blanquism made their situation difficult in theoretical debates.

MILITARY-REVOLUTIONARY ORGANIZATION

Events in the summer of 1906 made the arguments for decisive action to spark an insurrection seem even stronger. Military organizations were already in existence, and when military uprisings and mutinies broke out in July there seemed to be cause for optimism. Violence in the countryside continued, and it appeared that another revolutionary opportunity might be materializing. The moment for action could not be allowed to pass – revolutionary sentiments being expressed through the actions of soldiers and workers had to be supported by the Party.

Even before the Fourth Party Congress had met, several of the stronger Military Revolutionary Organizations of the RSDLP had tried to coordinate their activities by holding a conference. It was scheduled for mid-March, 1906, and was to be held in Moscow. Delegates from St. Petersburg, Warsaw, and Vilna were invited to join the Moscow delegates. However, an agent-provocateur had infiltrated the Moscow group, and the police descended on the first session, arresting the delegates and confiscating their revolutionary materials.[31] While this may have set back the Party work within the military it did nothing to remove the causes for unrest in the military. As the Social Democrats noted at the Fourth Party Congress, the government was having difficulty because it had not yet initiated needed reforms.

While the revolutionaries liked to think that unrest in the military sprang from the continued requirement for troops to quell uprisings, it appears that this was not exactly correct. An analysis of the places where military discipline disintegrated would have shown the Marxian theorists that economic determinism, rather than class struggle, was the critical factor.

A technological revolution had forced major changes in fortresses and their armament. The small brass and wrought iron muzzle-loading cannons of the 1850s had been replaced by enormous steel rifled guns. These new breechloaders had sophisticated recoil systems and fired large charges of smokeless powder. They fired high velocity projectiles which could pierce the armor of new battleships joining the fleets of the day, and they were truly wonders of modern technology. The new battleships mounted guns having equally destructive effects, and the old masonry walls of fortresses had to be replaced by reinforced concrete and earthworks. Both guns and emplacements were extremely expensive, and there was little money left to improve barracks. The fortress at Kronstadt exhibited the effects of this trend. It had been a showplace during Nicholas I's reign, but by the time Nicholas II assumed the throne living conditions had become virtually intolerable.[32] Just as the needs of industrial workers were subordinated to the machines they served, the living conditions of soldiers and sailors were subordinated to the requirements of the weapons they manned.

Physical discomfort was accompanied by poverty, with the low pay of the period leaving the enlisted soldier with no money for luxuries.[33] An already intolerable situation was made even worse by the exploitative tendencies of commanders who manipulated payrolls, ration funds, and fodder accounts for their own financial benefit. The situation was explosive, and the outbreaks of violence which occurred in 1906 should have been no surprise.

The first major disturbance erupted in the Sveaborg garrison in mid-July. A sapper unit confronted the commandant with a number of demands concerning living conditions and command relationships. They were promptly arrested and imprisoned, but this aroused the artillerymen, who, under the leadership of an officer who was a member of the SD Party, demonstrated against the garrison commander and mobilized a local workers' "Red Guard" unit. Repression was almost immediate, with the police and cossacks being assisted in this task by local townsmen who arrived in street cars carrying their Mausers and Brownings.[34]

The Sveaborg uprising, while unsuccessful, seems to have been the proximate cause of an uprising at Kronstadt. There had been unrest in the Kronstadt garrison because of the policies of the commandant, Admiral Chukhin, who had insisted upon strict discipline and had been a stickler for details in his day-to-day administration of the fortress. The situation did not come to a head until after the news of the Sveaborg uprising had been received. Then the crisis developed rapidly as a large portion of the garrison overpowered their officers and took over major sections of the fortress. Aroused by the sound of gunfire and by rumors from the fortress, the people of the town took to the streets and began building barricades. However, no coordinated effort to consolidate the victory followed these initial gains: the arsenal was not taken, the insurrectionists in the fortress did not establish ties with those in the town, and the remainder of the fortress left untaken contained enough troops and artillery to restore order. The outbreak was suppressed with great bloodshed, many of the sappers were captured, charged with being the instigators, tried summarily, and shot.[35]

Similar outbreaks in fortresses and naval vessels followed in late July and August, but they all ended in defeat. By early autumn it would appear that there should have been little cause for hope in the revolutionary ranks, but in fact there was a feeling of cautious optimism as the revolutionary potential of the military was analyzed. The capture of some of the leaders of the military committees had not ended their activities, and the uprisings, while unsuccessful, were seen as evidence of the revolutionary spirit which continued to burn in the breasts of the soldiers. Both the Mensheviks and the Bolsheviks were convinced that further Party activity within the military could lead to great success.

The Mensheviks put great hope in the formation of the "Union of Officers of the Russian Army". This was to be a non-party grouping of officers who shared liberal views, pledged to work together to improve conditions within their areas of responsibility while developing plans for improving the army as a whole. The successful growth of this group would challenge the supremacy of the traditional army officers whose answer to any form of unrest within the military was the enforcement of tighter discipline. The "Unionists" would respond to the legal complaints of their soldiers, allow them access to newspapers, and give them the freedom necessary to develop political consciousness. When this occurred, the army would no longer be a threat to the people.[36] In the interim the mere presence of such sentiments in a few army officers gave rise to hopes that the work of the military committees authorized by the Fourth Party Congress could proceed rapidly if properly organized. With this hope in mind the Menshevik-dominated Central Committee authorized a conference of military organizations to be held in October of 1906.

The actual proceedings at this October conference are virtually impossible to reconstruct because the Bolsheviks boycotted it and held a conference of their own in November.[37] However, reconstructing the proceedings from the partial protocols and Lenin's polemic against the October conference indicates that the Menshevik delegates primarily concentrated on organizational work among the officers and propaganda efforts within the ranks.[38]

The emphasis was placed upon developing organizations which would raise the consciousness of the troops so that they would not stand in the way of the masses when the revolution began.

Lenin may have been correct in expressing his dismay at the cautious limits inherent in such an objective. Evidence indicates that organizations of this sort already existed. Not only were they sending delegates to conferences, they were also producing propaganda designed to do exactly what the Mensheviks hoped. In St. Petersburg the military organization was publishing a newspaper, *Soldatskaiia Mysl'*, by October. This organ appears to have been well-conceived, and while its effect within the army cannot be measured, its propaganda impact certainly must have been appreciable. Its second number included an excellent revolutionary poem with a meter that would make it a good marching song. Entitled "Death Song" ("Predsmertnaia pesnia"), it told the story of the Kronstadt sappers who had been involved in the July uprising. As they dig their graves before they face the firing squad, the commandant taunts, "Dig, dig, dig – you wanted land and here it is; you'll have freedom too if you get to heaven". This callous attitude of the officer is nicely contrasted with the justice of the soliders' cause, and the power of such a propaganda device upon even a semi-literate soldier must have been considerable.[39]

In addition to its newspaper the St. Petersburg military organization was also publishing leaflets. An example is their rather detailed analysis of the domestic situation "On internal war" ("O vnutrennei voine"), which appeared in September 1906.[40] Specifically directed at the military audience, this leaflet asked the soldiers why they were not allowed to receive letters from home before they had passed through the hands of the censor. "Doesn't it appear that the government is trying to keep you from discovering that all of Russia is aflame? They are trying to make you think that you are only fighting isolated terrorists, but you are really resisting the will of the Russian people".[44] After discussing the failures of the government and the monetary and human costs of the Russo-Japanese War, the authors went on to discredit the Duma, pointing out that it had passed two laws dealing with the soldiers – both prescribing sentences at hard labor for various forms of revolutionary activity. Then they asked a series of difficult questions: Why shouldn't the soldiers revolt since they get nothing but fine words and an occasional medal for their work while the officers do nothing and get rich? Whose side will the soldiers be on when the armed rising occurs? Will they defend corrupt bureaucrats or join the workers and peasants who seek justice through the only available means?[42]

As a result of practical considerations springing from this apparent adequacy of existing organizations in accomplishing tasks defined by the October conference, Lenin's reluctance to follow the Mensheviks' lead, and his interest in questions of partisan warfare in the autumn of 1906,[43] it should not be surprising that the Bolsheviks had different objectives in mind when they met at Tammerfors in November.[44] In Lenin's words, their tasks were:

> (1) to devise concrete and specific steps which will enhance the chances of successfully propagating an uprising;
> (2) to prepare all possible technical means which can contribute to the success of an uprising;
> (3) to organize cadres of workers centered on the RSDLP, for active revolution;
> (4) to provide leadership for the democratic-revolutionary elements of the population, strengthening them through the fighting guidance of the Social Democrats.[45]

The small group[46] of delegates did what they could to accomplish these goals. The unrest in the armed forces had convinced them that the government's ability to respond to revolutionary threats had been significantly curtailed. They asserted that revolution in Russia was about to enter a new phase which would be characterized by much larger armed clashes between revolutionary and tsarist forces. In this situation the interests of the masses would be best served by the leadership of the Party acting as the vanguard, protecting the people from factionalism and opportunism while maximizing the efficiency with which revolutionary resources were employed. With this in mind, the delegates agreed that the Party had to expand and strengthen its organization within the democratic masses, but at the same time it had to erect organizations prepared to lead the armed uprising (the fighting organizations) while developing organizations having influence within the armed forces (the military organizations).

The first task was not one of the fundamental responsibilities of the delegates at the Tammerfors Conference, and it was not discussed in the formal sessions. The problem of the fighting organizations received careful consideration. The conference decided that these groups should first concentrate upon spreading the idea of armed uprising among the masses so that they would be better prepared and more easily mobilized when the moment for the uprising came. As this work progressed the fighting organizations would naturally identify workers who were the most enthusiastic supporters of armed uprising, and these men could be drawn into cadres which would actively participate when the uprising erupted. These men could be organized and trained, and the fighting organizations would then provide them with the weapons they would need. This procedure would allow the fighting organizations to maintain close control over their recruits, checking their loyalty and suitability before risking any part of the limited SD arsenal by placing it in unreliable hands. Success in these efforts toward organizing, training, and equipping the cadres would then tend to establish the leadership of the RSDLP in the minds of everyone who was seeking to promote the armed uprising. When the uprising actually occurred the fighting organizations would assume the leadership of the masses, providing both technical and tactical guidance.

Because many of the delegates were veterans of earlier uprisings, they had insights into the realities of violent situations that went beyond doctrinaire statements of Party leadership. Noting that suspicion among parties had not been fully overcome when insurrections began, but also recalling that enthusiasm among the masses had produced great numbers of volunteers seeking ways to help the cause, the delegates recommended that the fighting organizations set up information bureaus separate from the party units having activist roles. These bureaus would serve as clearing houses channelling the revolutionary energies to accomplish SD objectives while developing in newly-committed workers the habit of looking to the SD leadership for guidance. They would also serve as focal points for the propaganda effort designed to marshal even greater mass support for the armed insurrection. Information bureaus and fighting organizations working together would lead the masses to revolutionary victory.

Having defined the responsibilities of the fighting organizations, the delegates turned their attention to the military organizations. The primary task for these groups working within the armed forces was to be the erection of a pervasive Party organization having cells in every military unit.[47] When these Party organizations had been formed they could begin to identify sympathizers in the unit who would help to bring it over to the side of the revolution when the armed uprising occurred. The delegates expressed their confidence that proletarian elements in the army, just as in the rest of society, had the most advanced political consciousness.[48] As a result they were convinced that SD programs would enjoy great success in gaining the necessary activists who could lead the less enlightened men in the ranks away from the errors of their commissioned leaders when the proper moment arrived. In that period after the armed struggle had begun the military organizations would do everything they could to confuse and weaken the army while exerting maximum effort to gain control of their units.

Since this program of action for the fighting and military organizations was extremely ambitious, the delegates agreed that a central agency would be needed to control and coordinate the efforts of the numerous committees. They formed a "Temporary Bureau" to handle these responsibilities.[49] This bureau would not only coordinate activities; it would also provide communication with the Central Committee of the Party, develop technical doctrine for use in the forthcoming uprising, and supervise the publishing efforts of the military and fighting organizations. The first task of the press element was the widespread promulgation of propaganda *within the Party* on the subject of preparation for an armed uprising. Additional projects included the publication of newspapers modeled on the St. Petersburg *Soldatskaia Mysl'* to attract readers in the armed forces by providing fiction and poetry as well as news and editorial comment. Specialized tracts on military problems were also to be published for support of specific points in the Party program. The costs of this rather extensive publishing venture were to be defrayed by expropriation, which had been declared acceptable by the delegates.

When the Tammerfors Conference adjourned after a week of deliberation its participants could look back upon a number of accomplishments. They had erected the organizations which would enable the proletariat to engage in a victorious open battle with the armed forces. Having done this, they could advocate the Party's support of insurrection and end the cautious attempts to work within the system. They had openly challenged the guidance of the Fourth Party Congress, and they had thus laid the groundwork for the Fifth Party Congress' discussion of the role of armed action in future revolution.

MILITARY-REVOLUTIONARY QUESTIONS AND THE FIFTH PARTY CONGRESS

While the delegates met at Tammerfors, Trotsky sat in prison in St. Petersburg awaiting deportation to Siberia. But by the time the Fifth Party Congress met in May he had made his dramatic escape and had been greeted warmly by both Martov and Lenin.[50] With his ideas already beginning to form, he now joined the meeting which had begun in his absence and was continued in London.

The Fifth Party Congress was not an effective forum for the

discussion of military issues, however. The hostility between Mensheviks and Bolsheviks which limited the value of debate in many areas was especially virulent when the subject of military organizations was addressed. Lenin's expropriation squads were still operating in Russia in spite of the restrictions imposed at the Fourth Party Congress. Menshevik spokesmen characterized the Bolshevik activity as *Narodnik* terrorism and blocked the acceptance of the Bolshevik resolution on partisan warfare.[51] This resolution had been written to overcome these and earlier charges of Blanquism and set forth a program which might have been acceptable.

Taking into consideration:

(1) That at the present time the forces of the Russian revolution are insufficient for a victorious nationwide uprising.

(2) That given this lack of the necessary economic and political preconditions for a successful mass rising, the necessity for separate partisan acts against agents of political and economic repression must be recognized.

(3) That the organization of partisan insurgent detachments in Social Democratic groups should be acceptable, if only in this time when mass struggle is impossible.

(4) That on the other hand, in this period of relative calm, partisan uprisings will necessarily degenerate into anarchistic acts, weakening the Party in its struggle against anarchistic agitation within the working class and bringing demoralization to the Party's supporters.

(5) That armed groups formed by Party committees taking part in partisan struggles under the conditions of the present moment inevitably will be converted into secret conspiratorial circles, isolated from the masses and, being demoralized, will bring disorganization to the Party's ranks.

Taking all this into consideration, the Congress declares:

(1) That at the present time, lacking the strength for a mass revolutionary appeal, partisan uprisings are undesirable, and the Congress recommends an ideological campaign against them.

(2) That it is still possible that under conditions of mass revolutionary struggle, partisan uprising may be undertaken, but only through the initiative of the Party Committee, after a

decision of the central organ and with its strict control.

(3) That the form of armed organizations will closely correspond to the aim of preparing a fighting vanguard for the proletariat in the armed uprising, and will be a system of party militia which carries out the military training of all members of the Party within the limits of the authority of the Party cell.[52]

This resolution reflected Lenin's commitment to strict Party discipline, while revealing his continued belief in preparing the armed detachments necessary to lead any uprising which took place in the proper economic/political context. It also left room for leadership action which would allow the Party to prove it was on the side of the workers if an uprising should occur, even if it had little chance for success and had occurred in spite of Party propaganda designed to prevent its outbreak.

The Bolshevik resolution was far too adventuresome for the Congress to accept, however. The majority of the delegates seemed to be convinced that partisan activities should be avoided at all costs for they had become the means used by the authorities to justify repressive activity. Having passed a resolution calling for continued emphasis on agitational work within the armed forces as a means of weakening the agencies of repression, the Congress proceeded to declare itself opposed to Lenin's proposal:

Taking into consideration:

(1) That under the stress of acute economic conflict, the current unworkable and bloody politics of tsarism push certain strata of the proletariat into fighting to make a partisan uprising, i.e., staging individual and group revolts against the agents of government and the bourgeoisie.

(2) That in connection with this, the expropriation of public and private property has become more prevalent.

(3) That these anarchistic methods of struggle bring disorganization to the ranks of the proletariat, obscuring their class consciousness and engendering within them the illusion that individual action can be substituted for individual sacrifice to the needs of the mass uprising.

(4) That, in addition, the partisan actions and expropriations are justification used by the government for their repression of the peaceful population and the agitation of the Black Hundreds among the workers and soldiers.

(5) That participation of Party members in partisan actions

and expropriation not only limits the Party in its struggle against anarchistic tendencies in the working masses but also compromises it in the eyes of the popular masses and brings demoralization to its members.

Taking all of this into consideration, the Congress resolves:

(1) Party organizations must carry out an energetic campaign against partisan uprisings and expropriation, showing the working masses the complete bankruptcy of these means and the harm they do to the revolutionary cause in the struggle for the political and economic interests of the working class.

(2) Members of the Party will not participate in partisan or expropriation activities. Not having previously defined the forms of organization of the armed mass in the period of the armed uprising or for the task of self-defense, the Congress resolves that *druzhini* set up by Party organizations for special militant functions cannot serve the interest of the workers and can in fact only be used for terroristic tactics in a revolution and seem to be oriented toward expropriation. In view of this the Congress resolves that all special fighting organizations available to Party organizations must be disbanded.[53]

Now a loyal Party member could no longer take part in the organization of a military vanguard.

Trotsky's attitude toward this development cannot be reconstructed with any assurance of accuracy. He did not go on record in opposition to the Party resolution, but the degree to which he supported it is not clear.[54] Deutscher stresses the fact that Trotsky was preoccupied with articulating his theory of Permanent Revolution at the Congress.[55] This seems to have limited his willingness to become involved in the minor issues which were solidifying the schism in the Party, and he appears to have left the Congress without having clarified his opinions on the proper role of organized military cadres in securing revolutionary victory.

Since Trotsky was attempting to gain converts to his notions of Permanent Revolution he probably was presenting views similar to those he had set forth in his pamphlet, "Results and Prospects".[56] He had touched upon the military question several times in this initial attempt at stating the case for his new theory, and the tone of his comments indicates that he would have been in support of the Congress resolution against partisan activity.

In this pamphlet Trotsky argued that the real key to revolutionary victory was an armed populace. He expressed his disapproval of programs which relied upon the initiative of fighting organizations when he wrote:

> Only old-fashioned Blanquists can hope for salvation from the initiative of conspiratorial organizations which have taken shape independently of the masses; their antipodes, the anarchists, might hope for a spontaneous, elemental outburst of the masses, the end of which no one can tell.[57]

Instead, Trotsky argued, there was no hope for victory until the proletariat could "*understand* that there is no way out for it except through socialism: it is necessary that it should combine in an army sufficiently powerful to conquer political power in open battle".[58]

Speculating on the time at which the consciousness of the proletariat would be adequate to carry out this task, Trotsky wrote:

> it is of course true that the growth of political consciousness depends upon the growth of the numbers of the proletariat, and proletarian dictatorship presupposes that the numbers of the proletariat will be sufficiently large to overcome the resistance of the bourgeois counter-revolution. But this does not mean that the 'overwhelming majority' of the population must be proletarians and the 'overwhelming majority' of the proletariat conscious socialists. It is clear, of course, that the conscious revolutionary army of the proletariat must be stronger than the counter-revolutionary army of capital, while the intermediate doubtful, or indifferent strata of the population must be in such a position that the regime of proletarian dictatorship will attract them to the side of the revolution and not repel them to the side of its enemies.[59]

When this favorable balance of forces had been achieved, the proletariat could gain control of the state.

However, while consciousness of the need for a socialist revolution was a necessary precondition for revolutionary victory, it was not sufficient in itself. Weapons would be needed in that open battle with the forces of counter-revolution, and it was for this reason that Trotsky wrote:

> A civil militia, which was a class demand of the bourgeoisie in 1848, is, in Russia, from the very first a demand for the arming of the people and above all the arming of the proletariat. The fate of the Russian Revolution is bound up with this question.[60]

Yet at the same time Trotsky recognized "that in the hearts of our democrats the fear of the armed proletariat is greater than the fear of the soldiery of the autocracy".[61] If this was true there seemed to be no hope for revolutionary victory, for surely the autocracy would not take the fatal step of arming the workers that even the Russian liberal elements had resisted during the revolution of 1905. How, then, was a successful revolution to begin?

The answer to this crucial question was found in the military system of the time. All of the European Powers had come to rely on mass armies, which, by their very nature, placed arms in the hands of the workers. However,

> Having placed huge masses of men under arms, the bourgeois governments are unable to cut with the sword through the tangle of international politics. Only a government which had the backing of the nation whose vital interests are affected, or a government that has lost the ground from under its feet and is inspired by the courage of despair, can send hundreds and thousands of men into battle. Under modern conditions of political culture, military science, universal suffrage and universal military service, only profound confidence or crazy adventurism can thrust two nations into conflict.[62]

Conflict was inevitable, and whenever it occurred it would be fatal to the existing order. Having no military or political objectives which could outweigh the class consciousness of the proletariat in uniform, the Powers would be unable to motivate their armies in the field and "a European war inevitably means a European revolution".[63]

With this view of things to come forming his attitude toward the Party debates over military organizations, it is little wonder that Trotsky played a minor role in the discussion. The conclusions reached at the Fifth Party Congress were generally in agreement with his program for they recognized the critical role to be played by armed confrontation in the actual seizure of power. Yet at the same time the Party was doing very little to prepare for this armed clash. Trotsky could concur in this decision because he was convinced that the governments themselves would train the proletarian militia which would seize the inevitable victory. Now the proper thing to do was to wait for the imperialist conflict which would spell the end of the old order.

CHAPTER FOUR

Trotsky Reports the Balkan Wars

Waiting for the development of revolutionary preconditions proved to be more difficult than Trotsky had expected, and prolonged existence in the émigré circles of central Europe became extremely galling. In his autobiography Trotsky recalled the difficulties he experienced in coexisting with the "flower of the pre-war Austrian Marxists" whose conversations seemed to reveal "either undisguised chauvinism, or the bragging of a petty proprietor, or holy terror of the police, or vileness toward women. In amazement, I often exclaimed, 'What revolutionaries!'"[1] Many years later, when writing of those days in Vienna, Trotsky could scarcely conceal his incredulity. "These men, it seemed, believed neither in revolution nor in war".[2] However, the political freedoms which engendered this placid attitude in Vienna also allowed Trotsky to undertake the publication of a Russian language newspaper, *Pravda* ("The Truth"), designed to be smuggled into Russia to stimulate revolutionary fervor among the workers.[3] He also became deeply involved in the intra-party squabbles which persisted in spite of the passage of time. His efforts to serve as a unifying force produced no tangible results, and in the summer of 1912 he welcomed the chance to report the Balkan situation for the readers of *Kievskaia Mysl'* ("Kievan Thought").[4]

Trotsky had made several trips to the Balkans since 1910, and he kept himself reasonably familiar with political events there since he felt that the Balkans were a genuine "Pandora's box" with their potential being stifled by Great Power insistence on the maintenance of the status quo.[5]

The political issues which first attracted him to the Balkans centered on the "Young Turk" revolt of 1908 and the Austrian annexation of Bosnia and Herzegovina in the same year. The Young Turk movement promised a revitalization of the old Ottoman Empire based on constitutionalism and Turkish nationalism. However, the nationalist movement overlooked the tradition of autonomy for subject nationalities within the Empire. Balkan nationalities resented the imposition of Turkish customs and culture after their own national aspirations had been awakened, and strife between national groups and the Ottoman leadership became even more pronounced than it had been before the Young Turks' coup. A tragic situation ensued – the Young Turks seized power to halt the erosive forces of internal rebellion and Great Power intervention which were reducing the Empire's territory. Yet the Young Turks' victory accelerated the forces it was meant to impede.

The changed situation in Constantinople whetted the appetites of opportunistic elements in the Austrian and Russian governments. On 16 September 1908 the foreign ministers of the two states (Aehrenthal of Austria and Izvolsky of Russia) held a conference at Buchlau. They agreed that Russia would not oppose Austrian annexation of Bosnia and Herzegovina and Austria would not oppose the opening of the Black Sea straits to Russian warships. While Izvolsky sought Great Power support Bulgaria declared its independence from the Ottoman Empire (5 October 1908) and Austria proclaimed the annexation of Bosnia and Herzegovina. Faced with a *fait accompli*, Izvolsky was unable to rally the necessary Allied support, and Russia suffered extreme embarrassment in the ensuing crisis.

Serbia and Montenegro were disappointed by Russia's inability to act against Austria since both of these Balkan nations felt they had superior claims to the newly-annexed territories. Still weakened by the Russo-Japanese War, Russia could not intervene militarily and recognized the Austrian annexation in March, 1909.

In Serbia, Bulgaria, Greece and Montenegro anti-Austrian sentiment, fear of aggressive Turkish nationalism and a renewed sense of opportunism combined to stimulate a Balkan League in 1912. The Young Turk government still controlled affairs in Constantinople, but it was at war with Italy in Tripoli. The time was ripe for decisive war with Turkey, and on 30 September 1912 the Balkan states mobilized their armed forces.

As Trotsky moved to report on the wartime situation he recognized that the war was a reflection of the political and diplomatic issues which he had been watching throughout his Austrian exile, and he reported on these issues. But he also reported on military developments, and his columns reflect an awareness of military problems and a growing commitment to the use of conventional military force for revolutionary purposes.[6]

That Trotsky was able to develop his knowledge of military matters under the conditions imposed upon him as a reporter is quite remarkable. He never witnessed a battle and he was not even allowed to visit the front. Even in the Balkans military censorship of the press was well developed by 1912, and a balance had been struck between governments and reporters. The growth of popular daily newspapers had increased the appetite for news from the battlefront in the latter half of the nineteenth century and had led to the institutionalization of war correspondents, talented and innovative men who often exposed themselves to hardships and dangers to earn their pay and reputation by getting the exclusive stories that would increase circulation and gain the gratitude of editors.[7] But this activity, which earned the praise of editors and the acclaim of the reading public, was anathema to the general staffs of the armies being watched. Telegraphic communication made it possible for correspondents to file their stories rapidly, and if these accounts of the situation at the front were detailed and accurate, enemy agents could learn a great deal by merely reading the major newspapers of the day. Trotsky repeated the anecdote that epitomized this possibility: "It might be true as the story goes, that Moltke first learned of MacMahon's intention to relieve Metz by reading the Paris dispatches in the London *Times*".[8] Obviously government could not sit idle while war correspondents undermined their armies' ability to maintain the veil of secrecy necessary for the conventional conduct of war, and measures were taken to limit the possibility that a correspondent might compromise a military operation. These included reading proofs of domestic newspapers, clearing foreign correspondents' dispatches before they could be transmitted through telegraph facilities, and limiting access to front line areas.

All of these censoring measures were being used by the Balkan governments in 1912, and Trotsky, as a correspondent with a personal history of radicalism writing for a provincial newspaper having little influence on world opinion, was subjected to chafing restrictions. While he was granted several interviews with leading political figures, he was unable to talk with military leaders. His travel was limited, and he spent almost all of his time in Sofia and Belgrade.[9] Yet he was able to piece together remarkable accounts of the war. He frequented the coffee-shops where the war was being discussed; he kept his eyes and ears open when he was on the street; he interviewed wounded soldiers and officers; and he developed close friendships with correspondents from other newspapers.

These sources, when combined with his narrative genius and his ability to vicariously experience situations described by others, allowed him to overcome the censor's restrictions and not only write columns to fascinate the readers in Kiev but also to perfect his understanding of modern warfare. Serbia and Bulgaria were totally mobilized for the war, and with his cosmopolitan ability to fit comfortably into this new environment, Trotsky was soon analysing the enthusiasm of those who surrounded him. Belgrade and Sofia were congenial cities, and perhaps Trotsky was more capable of coming to understand war on their streets and in their coffee-houses than he would have been on the field of battle. The conclusions that he drew certainly could not have been more accurate. These can be divided into three categories for purposes of discussion: problems of societies at war, problems of strategy, and problems of tactics. In each area Trotsky developed generalizations and provided insights which illustrate his growing awareness of the technicalities of modern warfare.

PROBLEMS OF SOCIETIES AT WAR

While willing to grant that war might bring social and economic progress in the Balkans, Trotsky was extremely pessimistic about the prospects. His primary concern was the inevitable economic impact of mobilization, which he feared would offset any gains which might be made by force of arms. In his first column from the Balkans he described the problem:

> Serbia has slightly fewer than three million people. Three hundred thousand men are under arms. This represents one fifth of the male population, and the economic system of the country simply cannot bear the burden of the war.[10]

Even though hostilities had not yet begun when he was writing this column, Trotsky noticed that the inhabitants of Belgrade were encountering difficulties in their efforts to buy staple commodities. The mobilization decree of 30 September had already disjointed the work force, and it seemed to him that there simply were no workers available.[11] The harvest was virtually completed in the countryside, but how was grain distribution to be completed if war came? How could markets be sustained when most breadwinners were suddenly reduced to privates in national armies where they would earn little and produce nothing of value? It was clear to Trotsky that the consequences of war, even if hostilities were not prolonged, would be immense.[12]

When the war actually began he moved to Sofia and Trotsky noticed another economic problem which faced the belligerent nations. This was the immense cost of merely paying the enormous mass armies. In the Bulgarian case Trotsky estimated that

> The national bank can provide the government with nearly 80 million gold francs. Of this sum 10 million must remain on

deposit with banks in Paris and elsewhere abroad as collateral
.... For nearly four weeks the government had maintained
more than 360,000 men on active duty, and this could rise as
high as 450,000. The soldier's pay averages about five francs a
day. This amounts to a daily cost of about two million francs, or
sixty million francs per month! Even such rudimentary calcu-
lations reveal that Bulgaria and her allies cannot continue the
war for more than a month and must strive to conclude it in a
week.[13]

These economic considerations gave rise to the danger that the war
could not be successfully localized, for given the need for funds,
material, and foodstuffs, the temptation to turn to the Great Powers
for assistance would be enormous. Once the Powers had a financial
interest in the outcome of the war they could not be expected to
allow the nations they were backing to suffer reverses. Small defeats
might trigger intervention, and since the resources of the belligerent
Balkan powers were so limited a Great Power might be forced into a
precipitous act because of the time limits imposed by economic
realities.[14]

The Marxian background which had sensitized Trotsky to these
economic implications of the Balkan War had also developed
his awareness of the need for international class solidarity in progressive endeavors. In the eyes of many socialists the First Balkan
War appeared to be an indication that Marx's predictions were
coming true. The Balkan Federation was evidence of man's ability
to overcome petty parochial interests in the pursuit of higher ideals.
Narrow national and ethnic considerations were cast aside as Greek
joined Slav and Bulgarian–Serbian differences were forgotten in
the struggle with the common enemy. However, this wave of the
future seemed illusory to Trotsky. The total mobilization which
gave the war its stridency also reduced the spirit of international
solidarity. Trotsky did not argue that the war was not potentially
progressive, for he openly stated that "the defeat of the Turkish
armies meant more than a political change. It reversed the relations
of conqueror and serf; it promised a social revolution".[15] But while
admitting this, Trotsky could not agree with the Serbian socialist
who told him: "I am against war, but this war is a fact. At least we can
be happy that it is enhancing the brotherhood of the Serbian and
Bulgarian soldiers, for this symbolizes the brotherhood of the two
nations and will smooth the path to a Balkan federation".[16] Trotsky
saw nothing to guarantee the continuation of the friendship, but saw
instead nations converted into armed camps and asked the question

that seemed so obvious to him: "Is it not possible that one armed camp will turn against the other"?[17]

Events were to prove that this was a perceptive prediction even though it upset socialists at the time. Trotsky perceived the simple fact that war was becoming the accepted method of solving problems in the Balkans and that nations were risking their entire economies on the outcome of wars. Once this was the case, could they accept anything less than a total satisfaction of their expectations?

Trotsky had also noticed that the support for the war was not, in fact, rooted in the masses. Journalists supporting the war challenged this view by asking how mobilization could have gone so smoothly if the people did not favor the war. Trotsky countered this query with the assertion that failure to oppose mobilization is a long way from believing in a war. In Trotsky's view the war was merely a reflection of the aspirations of the ruling circles and was not being fought for things the people understood or would care about if they had understood.[18] Given these conditions, the solidarity between nations lacked substance, and close relations between the members of the Balkan Alliance could be expected to endure only as long as they served the interests of the ruling circles.

Trotsky noticed that a critical political problem sprang from this lack of popular support for the war. Mass armies could be effectively employed only if there was widespread enthusiasm. But the real issues which had engendered the conflict could not arouse enthusiasm. What difference did it make to a trolley conductor in Sofia if Adrianople became a part of Bulgaria? How would the life of a peasant in the Sava River valley be changed if Serbia annexed much of Macedonia? These territorial objectives only glorified the rulers – they did nothing to improve the lot of the common man. The peasant was willing to fight and even to die in a defensive effort to save his own village and his family, but why should he join an offensive and risk his life fighting for villages which would never be his, especially when in his eyes these villages were not as good as his own?[19] How then was he to be motivated to die for the government's goals?

In Trotsky's view this could only be done through playing upon irrational hatreds since there were no rational considerations which would mobilize the masses in an offensive war such as this. Hatred was the fundamental factor to be used in gaining support for the war. In his interview with Milorad Drashkovich, the director of the Serbian State Bank, Trotsky discovered that a crusade against the Turks was being preached. Drashkovich told him: "War against the

Turks has been inevitable for 500 years, and it will be inevitable until the Turks are driven out. We hope for success when war comes. We have faith in ourselves and in God".[20] The repressions suffered at the hands of Turkish landlords and bureaucrats had not been forgotten, and Trotsky did not doubt that these memories, together with the government's efforts to capitalize upon them, would serve as the emotional force which would drive the common soldier into battle.[21] But it was not difficult to foresee that the conflict which resulted would be savage and bloody in its totality.

This was the ultimate tragedy of the war. The ruling groups, in their pursuit of grandiose goals, were dissipating the lives and capital of their nations. Writing about the Bulgarian sacrifices, Trotsky summed up his position on the problems for society inherent in the war: "The redefinition of Balkan borders ... is being paid for by the retardation of the cultural development of this small country".[22] Progress, class solidarity, and capital accumulation were being destroyed by the ravages of war. By recognizing all of these social problems engendered by the First Balkan War in 1912, Trotsky was years ahead of his socialist colleagues who later hoped for progressive benefits during the First World War, but recognition could not alter them, and Trotsky's articulate opposition to war had no real effect in either instance.

PROBLEMS OF STRATEGY

Trotsky had never been placed in a position which forced him to analyse military strategy before he went to report the Balkan Wars. However, once he became a war correspondent he demonstrated remarkable ability in his analysis of the strategic situation. We have seen that Trotsky had few illusions about the societies engaged in the war and that he had no desire to romanticize the military experience. This gave his reporting a degree of dispassionate objectivity which aided him in his efforts at discerning the funda-mental relationships between military resources and the successful pursuit of governmental interests which are the essence of strategy. His recognition of the fact that a country's military resources are themselves the product of economic resources and political decisions increased his ability to weigh the feasibility of military alternatives while considering these more basic factors, thus developing conclusions in the realm of "Grand Strategy" where consideration of all factors which may influence the course of a campaign can render the campaign unnecessary or inevitably successful.[23] While Trotsky devoted most of his attention to describing the daily occurrences of the war, his approach to strategic questions made his occasional analyses of these questions extremely valuable and remarkably prescient.

One of the first tasks of the strategist is the determination of the decisive point. This is especially difficult in a war fought by a coalition since the member nations may organize their campaigns in response to selfish interests which contravene the rational principles upon which the theorist expects the coalition's strategy to be based. This problem was extremely complex in the First Balkan War since each nation had specific territorial objectives which it hoped to secure by military seizure. But the strategist seldom can consider the seizure of land to be the proper objective of a campaign. The enemy's army and his ability to resist the will of his opponent must be destroyed if any gains are to endure. Therefore the strategic analyst must look beyond the simple offensive victories in his attempt to determine the decisive point.

While Montenegrin attacks into Albania, Serbian operations in Old Serbia and Macedonia, and Greek offensives toward Salonika all were impressive, these were not the critical factors in determining the military results of the war. Trotsky knew this, and his knowledge was reflected in both his actions and his words. He was on his way from Belgrade to Sofia when the war began, moving to the capital of the nation which he knew would necessarily play the decisive role in the war. In an article written a few days later he explained the reasons for his actions.

> The political objectives of the war appear to be Macedonia and Old Serbia. But the main theater of military action must be the space between Adrianople and Constantinople. Therefore, the main burdens of the war must be borne by Bulgaria.[24]

He was now placed as well as he could be to analyze the effectiveness with which the Bulgarian army carried out its decisive role.

Trotsky had based his analysis of the decisive point upon several considerations. First, he argued that Constantinople was the real key to Turkish operations in the Balkans. If it was taken there could be no further Turkish resistance. If it was successfully defended, gains made elsewhere in the Balkans would never be secure until it had fallen. This meant that Constantinople was the ultimate objective of the Balkan armies.[25] However, a direct attack upon Constantinople was impossible: it was defended in depth with its defences occupying "the space between Adrianople and Constantinople", which Trotsky had defined as the critical area. If the Bulgarian army could neutralize these defenses it would be

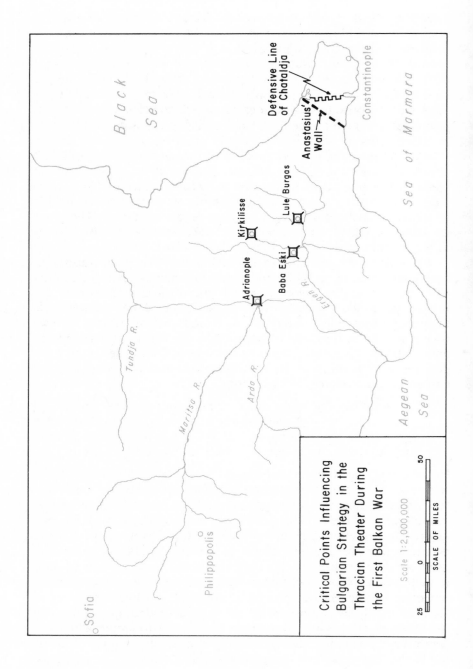

Critical Points Influencing Bulgarian Strategy in the Thracian Theater During the First Balkan War

Scale 1:2,000,000

SCALE OF MILES

victorious: if the Turks could defend them successfully they would be able to counterattack.

Having determined the critical point, the strategist must next determine the course of action to be followed if the desired outcome is to be achieved. Trotsky did this with great care, arguing that *time* would be the critical factor determining the outcome of the war. This assertion was based upon two considerations. The first was the economic situation in Bulgaria with which we have already become familiar. Trotsky was convinced that the Bulgarian army had to gain victory rapidly or the country would be faced with bankruptcy. The second consideration was more purely military, being a simple observation that the passage of time would allow the Turks to deploy reserves from the Asiatic regions of their empire against the Balkan nations. Since these nations were already fully mobilized, the balance of military might would gradually pass to the Turks as their reserves reached the critical theater. Since time was on the Turks' side, a successful Bulgarian strategy would necessarily be based upon rapid progress to a decisive conclusion of the war. The best strategy would be the one which maximized speed.[26]

The obstacles to be overcome in bringing the campaign to a speedy conclusion were numerous. Trotsky recognized that "according to the 1882 plan upon which the Turkish defenses were based, the road to the Bosporus and the Sea of Marmara was guarded by a four-cornered defense composed of four fortresses: Adrianople, Kirkilisse, Baba Eski, and Lule Burgas".[27] In addition he was aware of the fact that the Turks had developed a strong line of defensive fortifications across the peninsula at Chataldja.[28] His analysis of the proper strategic plan to be followed was inspired by the fall of the first of these obstacles, the fortress at Kirkilisse. Once this had occurred, it seemed to Trotsky that the time for investigating alternatives had arrived.[29] He discussed three possible courses of action. In the first the Bulgarians would reinforce their left flank units which had taken Kirkilisse and push forward immediately to take Constantinople. In the second they would reduce the fortresses of Adrianople and Lule Burgas and then move to attack Constantinople. In the third they would neutralize the fortresses at Adrianople and Lule Burgas with screening forces and use the remainder of their army to attack Constantinople after these screens had secured the right flank of the attacking force.[30]

The first plan appeared to offer the greatest speed, but it had some fundamental drawbacks. It required the Bulgarian army to operate with a formidable force threatening its line of communication,[31] and it also required rapid reinforcement of units operating in a primitive area where the communications network was already overtaxed. Organization and consolidation of the striking force might not proceed rapidly, and even if a force could be put in motion it would be dangerously exposed. Trotsky also was aware of the fact that the success of this operation would depend upon the nature of the resistance it encountered. If the Turks had not been soundly defeated at Kirkilisse but had instead retired in good order, the Bulgarian attacking force would find every river line and village along the few improved roads into Constantinople defended by the retreating Kirkilisse garrison. Such conditions would not favor the attackers, and Trotsky was convinced that these would be the conditions encountered.[32] He had been in Sofia when Kirkilisse fell to the Bulgarians and had heard exultant patriots gloating over "forty thousand prisoners, forty thousand rifles, hundreds of cannon, and millions of kilograms of provisions".[33] But if such spoils of war had really existed, representative samples would have soon appeared in Sofia to buoy up the popular support of war. All that ever appeared were a few Turkish prisoners, and there were no trophies, so Trotsky concluded that the Turks had retired in reasonably good order, leaving behind some sort of rearguard which the Bulgarians had captured. With this assessment of the enemy's potential for continued defensive operations against the Bulgarian left flank Trotsky felt that the first course of action, the rapid descent on Constantinople, would be dangerously rash.[34]

The second course of action, which called for full-scale attacks upon Adrianople and the remaining fortresses, was far less risky than the first, but it offered no genuine chance for Bulgarian victory because it would be extremely time-consuming. Attacking the fortresses would give the Turks time to transfer their reserves to defend Constantinople, and it probably would result in such a long siege that the Bulgarian government would be left bankrupt even if victorious. Finally, there was the possibility that the Turkish troops might be safely withdrawn from the fortresses after having delayed the Bulgarians for a prescribed period. If these forces then joined the reserves in the defense of Constantinople there could be almost no hope for a Bulgarian victory. With these considerations in mind, Trotsky concluded that the second course of action offered no real opportunity for success and rejected it.[35]

Having rejected the first two alternatives Trotsky felt that the third was the only approach worth trying. By screening Adrianople with "a large Bulgarian detachment ($1\frac{1}{2}$–2 divisions)"[36] it would be possible to neutralize the fortress while the main force continued the attack toward Constantinople. Speed and momentum could be maximized without totally compromising security, and with this plan the chances for victory might be quite good.[37]

But even with this plan there was a shortcoming. It gave no guarantee of success in the attack against Turkish defensive lines organized further toward the rear. Trotsky had studied his maps carefully and saw that it would be possible for the Turks to defend in depth, "taking up defensive positions along the line of the Ergen River or even further to the south along the wall of Anastasius in Chataldja, and await the arrival of their reinforcements from Asia".[38] If they adopted this course of action, the Bulgarians could gain a strategic victory only if they could successfully breach these lines. Trotsky was not sure that the Bulgarian army could accomplish this task. By late October he detected the growing Turkish concentration in Chataldja and asked:

> Can the Bulgarian army force this narrow gate? A Bulgarian politician who understands his country's capabilities and the realities of the Bulgarian–Turkish war told me, "The break-through of the Chataldja defenses seems to me to be a strategic impossibility. The Turks can use an army of fifty thousand there to block the advance of half a million". And the road to Tsargrad [Constantinople] must of necessity pass through Chataldja.[39]

Trotsky concluded that a bloody battle was inevitable and seemed to share his informant's view of its probable outcome.

A review of the actual events which followed the fall of Kirkilisse reveals that Trotsky's strategic analysis was remarkably accurate. The Bulgarians did in fact bypass Adrianople, covering it with a large screening force and preventing the escape of the garrison. However, the Bulgarian army wasted valuable time and resources attacking the fortress of Lule Burgas. While a great Bulgarian victory resulted on 3 November, this action contributed to the ultimate defeat of Bulgarian forces by the entrenched Turks defending the lines in Chataldja.[40] Working with limited resources Trotsky had derived the strategic plan and pointed out the critical areas which required special attention if victory was to be achieved. In retrospect Trotsky appears to have been a better strategist than those found on the Bulgarian general staff. He had a more perfect understanding of the need for speed rather than tactical victories, and he sensed the importance of massing forces in the critical theater rather than detaching troops to take political objectives.[41] In his discussion of strategy he certainly displayed a grasp of the fundamental priciples sufficient to allow valid analysis of complex military problems.

PROBLEMS OF TACTICS

Once society has mobilized its resources and a strategic plan has been developed for efficiently bringing those resources to bear against the enemy the forces which will bring men face to face on the battlefield have begun to operate. The resulting conflict, with its violence and finality, was the focus of the war correspondent's reporting. This was the real news from the front which fascinated distant readers, and Trotsky's columns on Balkan economics and strategic alternatives were vastly outnumbered by articles describing and analysing the actual struggles between the opposing armies. While this was the most fascinating news story the journalist could file, it was also the most difficult to construct because of the censor's restrictions. Trotsky outlined this difficulty when he wrote:

> Correspondents saw both a lot and a little; they observed the preparations for war and they saw the "products" of war: the wounded, the prisoners, the glow of burning villages; they heard the rumble of artillery fire. But they were not given an opportunity to accompany a maneuver element of the army and get an insider's view of an operation. Thus it is necessary to proceed by means of interviews, and to reconstruct a picture of the life and death of the army on the field of battle through the words of participants.[42]

The desire to "get an insider's view" seems to have been almost an obsession with Trotsky. He wanted to know what men did in combat and he seemed to hope that he might discover what combat did to men. His was not the idle curiosity of the observer but the passionate interest of the student. This should not be construed to mean that Trotsky had any sense of a future personal need to know the nature of warfare. This passionate interest in vital social problems was Trotsky's nature, and he studied war with the same consuming desire for knowledge that he had brought to his earlier contacts with economics, languages, and revolutionary theory.[43] Now he brought this commitment to understanding phenomena to his study of war, and he focused his attention on the individual soldier. This focus gave him powerful insights into the realities of the battlefield and colored all of his writings on the subject.

In fact, his focus on the individual was so complete in its application that it is perhaps inaccurate to discuss Trotsky's writings on actual battlefield events under the heading "Tactics". This word implies a science of moving and arranging combat resources in the presence of the enemy, and Trotsky was not committed to this notion that scientific truths prevailed. In one of his columns he quoted an experienced young officer as saying:

> In textbooks tactics are completely prescribed and pre-determined: the fighting element is here, the commander there, the hostile position a certain number of paces to the front, turning to the flank takes so many minutes. But none of this remains after the third, or perhaps even after the second day. I don't mean to say that the theory of tactics is a worthless thing. No; if there were no preliminary training all would be anarchy. It is in fact due to the inculcation of the elements of organization and order in the soldier that all of his chaotic primitive enthusiasms can be systematically preserved. But the disparity between the mathematical abstraction of the textbooks used in the schools and the living reality of movement in battle is enormous.[44]

Trotsky's writings indicate that he accepted this view as accurate, for he rejected the notion that battles were fought with mathematical precision, yet he also condemned the notion that there was a place on the modern battlefield for the soldier who lacked tactical training. This latter consideration is important since it explains Trotsky's denigration of the efforts of partisan groups which attempted to operate independently during the Balkan War or which served as auxiliaries to the Bulgarian and Serbian armies after having received arms and equipment. Because the members of these partisan bands were virtually ignorant of the conditions of modern warfare and were incapable of operating beyond the narrow limits of their chosen localities, Trotsky felt that they added to the misery war brought to the peasants without contributing to the decisive conclusion of the struggle.[45]

Trotsky was extremely interested in the potential of irregular warfare when he went to the Balkans. He had been sensitized to the problem of popular armed uprisings in 1905, and there seemed to be lessons to be learned in studying the actions of the Balkan partisans. Early in the war he devoted a long article to the *Chetniks* in which he attempted to analyse the significance of their revolutionary activity. In Trotsky's account the *Cheta* was a proud group of Slavic partisans who traced their resistance to Turkish rule back to the nineteenth century. They operated almost entirely in the mountains of Macedonia, where they enjoyed the support of the population and could safely evade Turkish patrols. The *Chetniks* had staged a major uprising in 1903 which had been followed by a four year insurgent struggle culminating in Turkish economic reforms which the *Chetniks* saw as a major moral victory. These reforms and the Young Turks' revolt, which occurred a few months later, bred an optimistic hope that armed conflict with the state was no longer necessary. Attempts to work within the system became the rule in the period 1908–1910, but Turkish leaders ignored *Chetnik* advice and the *Chetniks* began to fear that they were losing the confidence of the people. Revolutionary methods were adopted once more: *Chetnik druzhini* of five to ten armed men were set up in each district, and the mass organizations of supporters in the villages were rebuilt. Since the organizations were small and weak, a mass uprising was out of the question, but partisan activities (ambushing trains, robbing banks, and attacking government buildings) were initiated to remind the people of the Balkans and of Europe that the *Cheta* existed. When the war began the *Chetniks* continued to harass the Turks, and added sabotage acts such as cutting telegraph lines and ripping out railroad spans to their other activities.[46]

All of this sounds quite familiar, because Trotsky was essentially describing the same scenario he had postulated for continuing the Russian revolution after the failure of the December uprising in 1905: the masses organized to support armed detachments engaged in partisan activities which strengthen the revolutionary movement while weakening the government. But now Trotsky concluded that these methods could not be applied to the socialist revolution even though they might be suited to the Balkan situation. In the Balkans revolutionaries were still trying to complete the nationalist revolution. "Like Garibaldi in Italy they must gain the support of foreign diplomats to change the status quo, and this can be forthcoming if they are not challenging the stability of the entire arena in which those diplomats operate".[47] By making minor contributions to the war effort as partisans the *Chetniks* could hope to gain favors from the government of the victors, but their partisan activities would never be decisive in a military sense. With this conclusion Trotsky turned his back on the romantic Balkan revolutionaries and concentrated his full attention on the conventional armies. They would decide the outcome of the war, and their activities had to be analysed if the victory was to be understood.

Analysing the activities of the armies was not such an odious task. With the mobilization these were no longer professional military institutions. They were filled with working men even if they did not pursue objectives which workers would have chosen. Trotsky had been struck by this aspect of the situation as soon as he arrived in the Balkans. In a column entitled "First Impressions" (*Pervye vpechatleniia*), he had written:

> When I realized that more than a few men that I knew well, politicians, editors, and professors, were already standing at the border with rifles in their hands, ready to kill and maim in the forward lines – then war, that abstract notion which I had treated so lightly in my thoughts and words, became something beyond comprehension.[48]

In the same article he had brooded over the fates awaiting a shipload of reservists which his ferry had met as he was crossing the Danube to Belgrade. As the ships met, the soldiers waved their caps and cheered. Trotsky was shocked by their naive enthusiasm and could think only of the rivers of blood which soon would flow.[49] Because he was anxious to understand the impact of war on men such as these, he was forced to reconstruct many parts of the tactical "science" which he would not admit applied to the scenes he wished to describe. In his columns he described the movement to battle, the battles themselves with their mixture of primeval savagery of hand-to-hand fighting and the modern terror of long range artillery, and the problems of leadership which confronted the men who tried to maintain a semblance of order in the combat units. The picture which resulted was not one of red and blue rectangles following sharply defined arrows to meet in an abstract environment called war. Instead Trotsky depicted swarms of tired, hungry, and frightened men striving to accomplish the task that had been set for them.

Movement to battle was a subject that Trotsky saw as being just as important as the battles themselves, and he attempted to reconstruct it in his columns. He had experienced travel under arduous conditions in his trips to Siberia and in his famous escape of February 1907 when he had travelled 700 miles through central Siberia in a reindeer sled,[50] so he was able to understand the hardships the common soldier suffered. Trotsky recognized that even when a fight was not imminent the soldier's lot was not an easy one for he labored under a heavy pack, and his food was both scanty and poor in quality. In the case of the light infantry brigade of the Serbian army which Trotsky wrote about in some detail, loads ranging up to 25 kilograms (65 pounds) were not uncommon.[51] These troops were operating in the mountainous terrain of Old Serbia and Macedonia, and in addition to carrying such heavy packs they were required to manhandle howitzers over the worst parts of the roads because their unit had not been issued mountain guns designed for rough terrain.[52] Since supply wagons could not be dragged along, their food soon ran out and they were issued no bread for a week. When food was available the order to move forward often came before it could be cooked, and the men rapidly lost strength because of hunger.[53] Their movement was made even more difficult by the fact that their officers had few maps, and those that were available were illegible hectograph copies of badly out-dated Austrian maps. As a result units were often assigned routes on non-existent roads or found themselves tasked with moving heavy equipment along primitive mountain tracks.[54] But all of these obstacles were overcome, and eventually the army was able to advance far enough to give battle, even though Trotsky reported: "The soldiers say, 'What do the Turks have to fear from the Siberian army? It's a hungry rabble having neither bread nor pride' ".[55]

When battle was actually at hand the techniques of movement changed, and Trotsky's reporting reflected this. The Serbian army used almost no cavalry in mountainous terrain, so infantry skirmishers were sent forward from the main body to locate the enemy units and fix them in position so that they could be brought under artillery fire and then attacked by the infantry.[56] Trotsky reported that the Bulgarian army operating in the vicinity of Kirkilisse tried to use cavalry to perform this mission but mounted troops proved too vulnerable to the enemy's artillery fire and this practice had to be abandoned.[57] Trotsky's descriptions of this phase of action indicate his appreciation of the fact that battles began when the enemy had been located and artillery fire could become effective, not when the infantry units closed in final combat. Because he recognized this critical function of the artillery he devoted a great deal of space to analysing its effect upon the battlefield.

Artillery's most obvious effect was increasing the range at which casualties could be inflicted. In his account of Serbian battles Trotsky described a situation in which Serbian artillery neutralized an Albanian attack before the attacking unit had approached within 2000 yards of the Serbian main body.[58] He also noted that artillery was causing a high percentage of the wounds suffered by the combatants. Since he pieced together his columns by interviewing the wounded he had ample opportunity to collect data on this subject, and even though his accounts are impressionistic, he certainly was convinced that the technological advances applied to the artillery had resulted in enormous human costs.[59] At the same time he was aware of the fact that artillery was far from being the ultimate weapon. He reported instances when numerous artillery rounds injured no one because the unit firing them had not located its target accurately,[60] and he also noted that there were technological shortcomings in the weapons system. He cited cases in which as many as twelve rounds had fallen on a single platoon with no effect because the fuses had failed to function. Trotsky also reported that the bursting radius of the projectile fired by the Turkish medium howitzer was so great (as much as 100 meters) that it caused few serious casualties.[61] In addition, he was aware of the vulnerability of artillery pieces to the fire of enemy artillery. He recorded the complaints of a wounded soldier from the Bulgarian 16th Infantry Regiment who said that his unit, which had been given the task of providing security for an artillery site, had suffered more casualties than the other regiments in his division which had assaulted the Turkish positions. The Turks had been using their artillery to suppress the Bulgarian fire so that the Turkish infantry might be able to withstand the assault.[62]

Ultimately battle could only be won by infantry action, and Trotsky felt that when this began, rationality virtually ceased. Both sides in the Balkan War tended to rely on a frontal assault culminating in a bayonet charge as the decisive tactic. Given the presence of artillery, repeating rifles, and machine guns, these tactics resulted in bloody carnage, but no alternative had been found. Trotsky posited none, and he accepted this final savage clash as the real test of armies. Accepting it, yet recognizing its irrationality, he asked what sort of man could emerge as a hero in such a battle.

He found an answer in one of his hospital interviews, when he met a Bulgarian officer who had distinguished himself in this sort of hand-to-hand struggle. Having been wounded rather severely in the initial encounter, this man had staggered to the medical station for aid. While he awaited treatment word came that the Turks were breaking through. This officer rallied the other casualties in the aid station and led a counterattack which repulsed the Turks, during which he received several additional wounds. He told Trotsky:

> Military heroism in contemporary warfare must be a mass phenomenon. A soldier may make a heroic gesture, but it will mean nothing unless all the soldiers or the officers in the unit are heroes. It is only necessary that the goals of the army be known and that they be the goals of the soldiers; then heroism will emerge in modern wars.[63]

An answer such as this was not completely satisfactory. Trotsky wanted to believe that the army's values and the soldiers' values were not the same. What had happened to his friends who had been politicians, professors, and editors when they went off to war? Had they too fallen victim to the mass insanity of the bayonet charge when they heard the command, *"Na nozh!"*? If so, how could this phenomenon be explained?

The Balkan Wars were over before he could discover the answer. He had had an opportunity to develop his ability to analyse strategic problems while tempering the abstract skills of the strategist with human compassion for the men who carried out their plans. He had seen enough of modern warfare to conclude that partisan fighting could not be decisive, but he could not yet understand the psychology of the front lines. In a matter of months, with the outbreak of the First World War, he was to have the opportunity to continue his study of men's actions on the modern battlefield.

CHAPTER FIVE

Trotsky's Analysis of Military Matters during the World War

After reporting the Balkan Wars Trotsky rejoined the radical émigré community in Vienna. When war broke out again in August 1914 he was forced to flee. Even though he embraced internationalism and was considered a criminal by the Russian government, the Hapsburg bureaucracy saw in him a dangerous foreign national who might compromise the war effort. Warned of imminent arrest, Trotsky moved his family to Switzerland, where he stayed for only two months.[1] Settling in Zurich, he became involved in Swiss Labor politics but devoted most of his attention to a pamphlet entitled "War and the International" (first published in English as "The Bolsheviki and World Peace"). In passages filled with rage born of disappointment he condemned the socialists of the belligerent nations for their lack of devotion to international ideals. Yet he retained his commitment to the notion that the revolution was at hand, and he concluded by writing:

> We revolutionary socialists did not want the war. But we do not fear it. We do not fall into despair over the fact that the war has smashed the International, the old ideological–organizational form worn out by history. With the inexhaustible resources of proletarian socialism, the revolutionary epoch will create a new organizational form corresponding to the greatness of the new tasks. To this work we are applying ourselves amid the rattling of machine guns, the crash of old cathedrals, and the patriotic howling of capitalistic jackals. Amidst this hellish music of death, we preserve our thought in all its clarity, our vision remains unclouded, and we feel ourselves to be the only creative force of the future.[2]

These stirring lines were little more than empty bravura, however, for there was almost nothing left of the international labor movement in the autumn of 1914, and years later, even after he had been exiled from the Soviet Union, Trotsky recalled that the war credits vote of the German Social Democratic Party "remained one of the tragic experiences of my life".[3] Trotsky recognized the fact that building the new revolutionary organization would be a slow and painful process, and he seems to have welcomed the chance to have a new source of income and an outlet for his energy during this difficult period.

Early in November he had received an invitation to renew his relationship with *Kievskaia Mysl'* by becoming a war correspondent once again. Trotsky recalled:

> I accepted the offer from the paper all the more eagerly because it would give me a chance to get close to the war .... After the checking of the German advance on the Marne, the war became constantly more exacting and ruthless. In the boundless chaos that was enveloping Europe, with silence from the masses of workers, deceived and betrayed by the Social Democracy, the engines of destruction were developing their automatic power. Capitalist civilization was reducing itself to absurdity while it strove to break the thick skulls of men.[4]

Now the talents for analysing and reporting military affairs which had been developed during the Balkan Wars could be brought to bear upon a conflict which seemed to hold the promise of new revolutionary opportunities. Trotsky approached the journalistic task with the same enthusiasm he had displayed two years earlier, and the reports he produced displayed the same powerful insights into the complexities of a war which he could only observe from afar.

Trotsky not only wrote columns for *Kievskaia Mysl'*; he also joined the editorial staff of the Paris newspaper *Golos* (later renamed *Nashe Slovo* after a clash with the censor).[5] This gave him an opportunity to remain active in émigré politics, and it brought him into contact with Vladimir Alexandrovich Antonov-Ovseenko, who was a chief organizer of the newspaper.[6]

Antonov-Ovseenko was the son of an army officer who had become a Social Democrat while attending a St Petersburg cadet school. He was commissioned in the Imperial Army, but his military career was dramatically terminated when he led his detachment on the side of the insurgents in the Sevastopol uprising of 1905. He managed to escape to the West, where he became active in Menshevik circles.[7] Trotsky found in him a man with a rather sophisticated knowledge of military affairs who shared his conviction that the relationship between military events and the development of the revolution was critical. While the exact nature of their collaboration cannot be reconstructed; Antonov-Ovseenko's enthusiasm for columns on military topics opened the pages of *Nashe Slovo* to Trotsky's articles. Thus in the course of less than two years spent in Paris (Trotsky was ejected from France in October 1916 after a mutiny of Russian troops serving in France had been blamed on their exposure to *Nashe Slovo*[8]), Trotsky was encouraged to write several hundred pages of commentary on the war.[9]

Restrictions imposed upon journalists because of security considerations limited Trotsky's ability to make contact with participants in the war even more severely than had been the case in the Balkan Wars. Therefore, it is not surprising that interpretation and even speculation often predominate in his articles. Yet he was able to build upon chance encounters with soldiers in cafés and on trains, visits to wounded acquaintances in hospitals, and conversations with soldiers who shared his political views to write remarkable descriptive accounts of the war.[10]

Analysis of all of these articles reveals Trotsky's growing command of the technical complexities as well as the broader social implications of the horrible war on the Western Front. His grasp of the realities of the war seems to have been superior to that of many generals who were fighting it. In his columns the mature military thinker begins to emerge, and the superiority of his thinking derived from the span of his vision and his detachment is evident. Unlike most generals engaged in the war, Trotsky could see the war from many points of view, encompassing private soldier, small unit leader, military theorist, diplomat, and industrialist in his attempts to perceive the fundamental realities of the war. Trotsky was unhampered by the preoccupations of military responsibility which focused the generals' attention on the battlefield, and thus he could discern conditions ranging from economic capabilities to troop morale which had fundamental impact on the outcome of the war yet lay outside the field of view of his blinkered military contemporaries. The three general levels of inquiry which facilitated the discussion of Trotsky's writings on the Balkan Wars can be used once again, and in all three cases (Problems of Societies at War, Problems of Strategy, Problems of Tactics) Trotsky displays improved knowledge of military theory and practice.

PROBLEMS OF SOCIETIES AT WAR

From the very beginning of the war Trotsky was sure that the long-term result of the conflict would be revolution. However, he was enough of a realist to recognize that the failure of the Second International had deprived the working class of leadership, and he was convinced that in the absence of revolutionary initiative the war might drag on indefinitely. Therefore he devoted a great deal of attention to the impact the war was having on the societies which were engaged. Their economic, social, and political compositions all seemed to be fundamentally threatened by the demands of the war. The relationship between the war and economics appealed to Trotsky as it had during the Balkan Wars and he used his knowledge of economic realities to help explain the course the war was taking.

Trotsky arrived in Paris on 19 November 1914, and by that time the war had assumed a character predicted by very few military theorists. Europe had experienced a series of short, decisive wars in the half-century before 1914, and strategists in Germany and France planned for a larger but essentially unchanged scenario. Technological advances had given infantrymen machine guns and repeating rifles while improving the artillery's range, accuracy, and rate of fire. Before 1914 analysts were convinced that these technical advances favored offensive action. They combined this conviction with general staff expertise, industrial capability, and large reserves of trained manpower to produce offensive plans of unprecedented scope.

War erupted in Western Europe on the night of 4 August 1914 when the right flank of a German army of 1.5 million men attacked through Belgium. The French armies launched a massive offensive seeking a decisive breakthrough in the vicinity of Metz.

German forces advanced rapidly into Northern France while the French attack was repulsed in a series of large battles during the period 14–24 August (the "Battle of the Frontiers"). During the last week of August French troops shifted to meet the German threat against their left flank. French and British forces halted the German advance in the Battle of the Marne (6–10 September).

German forces withdrew to defensive positions behind the Aisne River, and the Allies mounted a succession of frontal attacks against these positions in the last two weeks of September. Each side made repeated attempts to outflank the other, and the resulting "race to the sea" ended in strategic stalemate. Lacking an assailable flank both sides launched numerous frontal attacks in the First Battle of Ypres, 12 October–11 November. The armies suffered heavy losses and made minimal gains. Neither side was prepared to capitulate, and there was no foreseeable end to the war that was to have been decided in a single campaign.

Trotsky argued that the initial military successes which Germany had enjoyed were quite easily understood:

> The military successes of Germany, it appears, are ultimately the result of a superior capitalistic organization. Military technique appears to be only an application of general techniques in the area of annihilating populations.[11]

This notion that war was simply a business having the destruction of humanity as its objective appealed to Trotsky. The modern general managed men and machines just as the capitalist did, and the general who had superior resources and employed these resources most efficiently would defeat his competitor just as surely as the capitalist would, given the same conditions. Trotsky's application of this analogy to capitalist competition gave him an important insight into modern warfare: the ability to employ machines was at least as important as the ability to employ men. Here Germany's superiority was obvious.

> In this war Germany set out as a powerful *industrialized* nation against Russia, having a predominantly *agrarian* population; as a *strong centralized* industrial country against France, having a small and only partially industrialized economic base; as a *modernized* and *rationalized* capitalistic nation against England, having an old *conservative* capitalistic structure.[12]

Germany's industrial superiority was thus a key to understanding the rapid mobilization and early victories of August 1914.

But these victories had not been decisive; the war had not ended, and in the long struggle which followed, Trotsky doubted that Germany could win the war. The question of victory was now a matter of human and industrial resources, and since the Allies had a superior reservoir of resources, they would eventually succeed in their war of attrition, wearing out enough German machines while killing enough German soldiers to gain the victory eventually.[13]

This assessment, made in 1915, ultimately proved to be an accurate prediction of the course the war was to follow. However, it should not overshadow the earlier assertion that it was *management* of economic resources which gave the Germans their initial advantage. Trotsky recognized the importance of the relationship between the men who managed its economy, and he argued that both the existence and the predominance of the former class were critical to an understanding of German successes.

The recognition of the existence of a professional military group

75

in Germany was nothing new. When Trotsky wrote of the Prussian Junkers his readers needed no footnote to explain the meaning of the term. Those readers understood both his purpose and his prejudice when he recounted the anecdote of Hindenberg out on maneuvers with his regiment "a quarter of a century ago" being invited by a young lady to join in an evening of music and literature. "He replied that he hadn't listened to music or read a literary work since his cadet days – he spent all of his time preparing for future wars".[14] Trotsky was convinced that men such as this were an important factor in the army's strength, quoting without refutation the pean of a conservative German professor:

> The primary portion of the army is that group of people who make military affairs their profession, who throughout their entire lives do nothing else and are constantly preparing for war, studying its art, its theory, and its practice. Only in this group does the military spirit thrive.[15]

There was little doubt that a professional military group existed in Germany.

The originality of Trotsky's analysis lay in his recognition of the fact that this group had the prestige necessary to control economic decisions so that their plans for war would be supported by the material realities of the society they sought to defend. Thus, Trotsky concluded his Hindenberg anecdote by noting that Hindenberg "has been made a Doctor of all four faculties at Konigsberg University",[16] in spite of his notable lack of interest in intellectual pleasures. But more important, the prestige reflected in decisions to award honors such as this had resulted in "feudal thinkers being invested with capitalistic resources"[17] for the pursuit of their war aims. In Trotsky's view, the explanation for this phenomenon was quite simple: "Germany is a country without France's revolutions".[18] Germany had undergone rapid industrial development without a bourgeois revolution, and as a result there was a unification of political and military power in the hands of the Junker group. This allowed them to turn the major impetus of economic development toward militaristic ends and put a modern military machine at the disposal of an old warrior caste.[19]

Trotsky went on to argue that the peculiar nature of Germany's economic development was a double blessing for the Junkers, for not only did their leadership within society remain unchallenged; the economic changes qualitatively improved the population from which their armies would be drawn:

Militarism is not simply cannons, searchlights, and blacked out automobile headlights; it is above all people. They kill and are killed, they put the mechanism of war into motion, and they do this with the greatest success when they are most closely involved with capitalistic techniques during peace time. Fifteen years ago the German press carried a long polemic on the relationship between the industrial development of the country and its military capabilities. Agrarian reactionary writers argued that the growth of industry was weakening the village and thus undermining the foundation of militarism, which essentially rested on the healthy, devout, patriarchal, and patriotic peasant. In opposition to this school of thought, Louis Brentano argued that only in the proletariat would capitalism find the cadre of a new army. Brentano was convinced that even in 1870 the best regiments had been the Westphalian, which had a number of workers in their ranks. In the Balkans many officers told me that worker-soldiers are not only more intelligent than peasants, but that they are also more adaptable and thus are more capable of tolerating the hardships and demands of war.[20]

Since 1905 Trotsky had recognized that the men behind the guns were as important as the guns themselves, and with this argument he was presenting the evidence that convinced him that German militarism reflected a superior combination of leadership, machines, and men which had emerged because of the nature of Germany's economic development.

But if the German military machine was superior, why had it failed to gain decisive victory in the first campaign? Trotsky's answer to this question was essentially based upon social rather than economic considerations, and it was based upon a consideration of French rather than German strengths. Trotsky noted that France, with its Republican government, had tried to limit the "feudal authoritarianism of militarism".[21] While the French Monarchists had frankly envied the German army, the Republicans argued that the French army ought to reflect the society — it should be a democratic militia in which every man defended his country. As a result, "A bastard regime has emerged in which the old and the new (the latter being epitomized in Jaurès' *L'Armée nouvelle*) have collided and have neutralized each other".[22] The conflict of these two ideas weakened the French army in the conventional sense: the professional cadre was smaller than it should have been, and it lacked social and political prestige. At the same time the reserves were large and unwieldy, being viewed by Republican enthusiasts as a militia in which every man would serve, even if such an objective was beyond the training capabilities of the regular army. As a result, the French army appeared to be no real match for the German army when the war began. However, once the conventional army held in the battle of the Marne, it was able to draw upon the spirit of the Republican concept, and that improved French chances for victory.

In Trotsky's estimate, the French army had never been as weak as it looked to conventional analysts, and the democratic notions which had limited its appeal during the pre-war period would be assets rather than liabilities in a prolonged war.[23] "The French, having been attacked, will now be able to settle into the military routine which was impossible in the days of peace, and they have more resources".[24] Having adopted the tactics of *guerre d'usure* (war of attrition), they had the advantage, for "those who advocate the war of attrition policy are essentially arguing that the side with the greater material and spiritual resources will win".[25]

But even the country with the greatest resources showed signs of tremendous strain during the war, and Trotsky felt that a fundamental social disjunction was developing. "In general terms", he wrote, "today's generation can be divided into two different parts: direct participants in the war, and passionate, captivated spectators of it".[26] Because the war was so horrible, he was becoming convinced that those who had not experienced it could never understand it, and those who had would become a class apart, recognizing their survival of the horror as a social bond more fundamental than any other. Trotsky's efforts as a war correspondent had sensitized him to this problem, for he feared that his own vicarious experience of the war was inadequate:

> the professional links between the army and the country, the military correspondents, give material which is essentially very dramatic and interesting, but unreliable in its psychological relationships to the majority of situations. This is primarily due to the fact that the correspondent must accomplish his task at long distance: the correspondent is not allowed to go near the lines, at least on the French Front. And even in cases such as this, when the correspondent is trying to convey reality, his work gives the reader only a glimpse of that gigantic process which is called war. Thus circumstances further contribute to the perpetuation of the psychological processes that spiritually isolate us from the war.[27]

By raising this issue Trotsky moved into exciting new territory, for he was attempting to analyse the social impact of the war. In the past, war correspondents had measured the damage of war in physical terms: the number of killed, wounded, and homeless; the destruction and pillage that marked the paths of armies. Now Trotsky was asserting that the survivors who suffer no apparent physical harm may be among war's victims and that society itself will be transformed, not only by the loss of those who are killed, but by the change it undergoes while surviving.

Trotsky attempted to investigate this problem by analysing the psychology of the soldier, a subject which had aroused his curiosity during the Balkan Wars. Now he renewed this interest in his attempt to understand the war, broadening his inquiry as the conflict had broadened in his effort to understand the social significance of the phenomenon he was observing. However, he expressed the fear that correspondents could not give a totally accurate picture of the war because they had their own political and national points of view. This, together with their desire to "sell" – to be dramatic and attractive – led them to transform accounts to fit their own pre-conceived notions of the real nature of the war.[28] He postulated that

> It might be possible to discover the real psychology of the war if, in the first moment of release, when they lack sufficient energy to hide their psyches, you could talk to officers or men who have spent several days under fire in the trenches, survived an artillery barrage, or just returned from an attack.[29]

Using these sources as a guide, Trotsky published the results of just such an interview.[30]

His conversations with soldiers had indicated that they were transformed by experiencing trench warfare, not by the training or patriotic speeches which filled their time before they were dispatched to the front. His respondent says: "When we set out we thought it was simply a maneuver and couldn't imagine the horrors, but we were soon exposed to them ... we left behind the fields and factories where civilized law applies and entered the area where the law of war prevails".[31] The nature of the war, with its immobility in the trenches, with the enemy only yards away, seemed to impose its own rules upon those who fought it. The fighting conditions changed men's material existence so fundamentally that their psychological make-up was transformed. "You don't live in a house, you can't walk along a street, you don't even have the amenities of life which can be expected by a soldier garrisoning a fortress".[32] Surroundings were dictated by the problem of survival, and as a result men were constantly preoccupied with improving the material defense which might save their lives. Deepening trenches, improving firing positions, and strengthening the overhead protective cover of bunkers all became acts of great significance which could devour hours and leave the soldiers exhausted from their efforts. Trotsky noted that "this helps overcome fear of the great danger by concentrating on the banal",[33] and he drew upon his own experience, likening it to the psychological tricks used by prisoners to maintain their self-control in the hostile and unchanging environment which surrounds them. But

> Ultimately the soldiers can think only of the Germans, and blaming them for the stink of war, they become a part of the instrument for its continuation. Nationalism, military glory, and imperial splendor are all empty notions. Journalists mistakenly think these are important – soldiers do not make this mistake.[34]

His own descriptions of the squalid terror of the trenches led Trotsky to conclude that this war was qualitatively different from all others. In former wars, in bivouac or in position, it had been possible for the soldier to get a better view of the military organization and what it was to do. Now that the armies had dug themselves into the ground to be invisible from their enemies, they had become invisible to their own members. There seemed to be no organization, but only a blind, irrational, and relentless force which was pushing men to their deaths.[35] In former wars, because of the nature of the bivouac, military life seemed to have been an extension of life at home. "Both at home and in the army the soldier felt himself to be in harmony with the elemental forces of nature. In both cases he responded to an outside force which guided his actions from birth to death. This was true whether he worked in the city or in the countryside".[36] If he was drenched or miserable in bivouac or hot and dusty on the march he seldom thought of blaming the enemy who was remote and unseen. When forces met on the field of battle it was a short encounter.

Trench warfare broke that continuum between civilized life and war by keeping the soldier so close to the enemy for such prolonged periods. Because it was so completely dehumanizing, and because so many of its miseries could be blamed on the enemy, it was not perceived as being an extension of normal existence. In the trenches man was being transformed by the horrors of war, and Trotsky concluded that society could never be the same again. The war had engendered social changes that would foster revolution when the fighting finally stopped.[37]

Trotsky's intentions in raising this line of argument are obscure. In asserting that participation in the war was the fundamental social determinant of the era, he appeared to be on dangerous ground as a Marxist. Did armies not bring together bourgeois, peasant, and proletarian elements? If these all came under fire together at the front, Trotsky's argument implied that they would form a social class from that time forward, with factory workers who became soldiers having more in common with the officers who shared their trenches than they had with the workers who remained in factories during the war.

This may have been his intention. These columns were written at the time of the Zimmerwald Conference (the conference was held on 5–8 September 1915, and the columns appeared in *Kievskaia Mysl'*, 11–25 September) when Trotsky was disturbed by the continued passiveness of the workers. In the Zimmerwald Manifesto he wrote, "Organized Workers! Since the outbreak of the war you have put your energies, your courage, your steadfastness at the service of the ruling classes".[38] The columns on the world of the trenches can be seen as an affirmation that those enormous masses who actually experienced the war would not be fooled by patriotic phrases and would lead the workers away from their chauvinistic errors. In August he had written in *Nashe Slovo*, "The war is pushing the working class toward Marxism as the only escape from their conditions".[39] It was only logical that soldiers in the trenches should be the first to feel the push.

The governments struggling to keep the trenches filled were also engendering social change as they sought to solve unprecedented wartime problems. Peacetime luxuries were set aside to facilitate the war effort, and this was as true in the political arena as it was in the marketplace. Trotsky addressed this aspect of the war's impact early in 1915:

The war has in fact abolished constitutional mechanisms, not only in Russia, but even in countries with ancient parliamentary traditions. The parties of the popular masses either voluntarily don the shackles of "national unit" or, as in the Russian case, handcuff themselves to the leadership of the Duma majority. Having gained freedom from all controls, even that which is simply criticism, the governmental machine sets out to simplify the transmission mechanisms between the producing population and the war's gaping mouth. Just as at the time of mobilization the railroad department was freed of all regulation and scheduling, so the governments of all belligerent nations, and Russia in particular, flout all rules of governmental behavior in time of war and rule with only one goal: the earliest possible seizure of the goods of this and future generations.[40]

Governments would continue to streamline their operations at the expense of personal freedoms as long as the war continued. But in spite of all these efforts to meet the demands of the battlefield, there still would be no prospect of victory. This led Trotsky to conclude that the political impact of the war was paradoxical: while it appeared that governments were becoming stronger as the war progressed, they were in fact becoming weaker.

The war seems to be the primary contradiction, the fundamental double-edged factor in historical development through which the revolutionary party, feeling the hardening of class conflict in the very soil beneath their feet and having faith in their future, can see the path to their political success. Defeat disorganizes and demoralizes the forces of reaction, but at the same time the war disorganizes the entire society, especially the working class. The war is not such an auxiliary factor that the working class can gain control over it: its tyranny must be removed before they can carry out their revolutionary tasks.[41]

This rather ambiguous approach was characteristic of Trotsky's writings on the political impact of the war. He had no clear revolutionary program designed to capitalize upon the confusion brought on by the war, and he was basically committed to the notion that the belligerent nations would have to end the war before the revolutionary situation could develop. As a result, it should not be surprising that he devoted some attention to the strategic problems inherent in the war, since he hoped that an understanding of these might lead to an appreciation of the conditions which had to be satisfied before the war could be ended.

STRATEGIC PROBLEMS

Trotsky began his analysis of strategy by examining the original German intentions and seeking the reasons for the German failure to gain a rapid victory. While we have already seen that Trotsky had great respect for the power of German militarism, he was not impressed with the war plan which the Junkers had evolved.

The German strategy, which reflected feudal thought implemented with capitalistic resources, called for a violent onslaught to destroy the enemies' active forces. This plan incorporated the entire German army ... and in the first week it seemed destined to succeed. But a great nation of today, with its enormous material reserves and a multi-million population composed of intelligent people capable of exercising initiative will not capitulate to a few hundred thousand well-armed men.[42]

From Trotsky's viewpoint it appeared that the German military leadership had demonstrated a complete failure to grasp modern realities. The "feudal" aspect of their thinking was reflected in their erroneous notion that a nation's strength lay in its standing army.

> It was believed that the army was composed of its regular cadre, with the entire remainder of the male population serving only as a raw or partially worked material which would play a secondary role in the reserves .... In fact the decisive part of the army is not the active formations but the reserves.[43]

The German theorists had failed to detect a qualitative change in the nature of warfare. They recognized that improved industrial techniques now made it necessary to employ a larger army, but they merely planned to repeat the decisive battles of the Franco-Prussian War on a larger scale. The Schlieffen Plan called for the encirclement and destruction of the active army, but in Trotsky's view, even if this plan had succeeded it would not have been decisive. The strategy failed to take cognizance of the political and economic strengths of France which would remain intact even if the army were destroyed in the field. Both national sentiment and industrial potential had been strengthened in the 40 years since the last German victory, and these could be employed by the French to resist the German invaders. Neither army understood the realities of modern warfare at the beginning of the war, and the limited vision of decisive objectives which led both General Staffs to concentrate on destroying the enemy's army was clearly inadequate for victory. Trotsky therefore showed no surprise when he reported that

> The grandiose German attack on the Yser River (which led to the Belgian decision to flood their sector and clearly marked the end of the "Race to the Sea") had no real results; one wall stands against another, and military operations have come to a dead end.[44]

The stalemate reflected the economic and technological balance between the foes, and Trotsky felt that it was a strategic inevitability. When attempts were made to open new fronts he had no reason to expect that they would break the stalemate, and in August 1915 he reported laconically that "on Gallipoli, just as on the new

Austro-Italian front, the lines of trenches serve to underline the hopelessness of the military situation".[45] Because either side could prevent a breakthrough, "Decisive results are not being achieved in a single theater".[46]

But if the military stalemate was a reflection of economic and technological balance, it seemed obvious that there might be possibilities for a decisive change in the strategic situation if this balance could be upset. In the Zimmerwald Manifesto Trotsky had written, "All science, the work of many generations is devoted to destruction".[47] Now it seemed that science might provide the breakthrough to end the war. While generals scanned their terrain boards looking for a physical weak spot that could be exploited to break the stalemate, Trotsky studied the battle reports to find a technological weakness that could be similarly exploited.

Trotsky was optimistic about the prospect of a technological breakthrough. He argued that European militarism had been developing all the tools of war made possible by the growing sophistication of capitalism. Some observers had noted the growing destructiveness of the new weapons and had remarked that they were making war absurdly expensive and therefore impossible. Trotsky merely observed that "war has become monstrous, but it has not become absurd", and argued that the old theories of strategy and tactics had become outmoded by this rapid technological change while new theories to cope with the "automated warfare" had not been evolved.[48]

In an article on "War and Technology" (*Voina i tekhnika*) written in December 1915, Trotsky outlined the basic problems and contemplated some possible solutions. He pointed to the fact that all European nations, no matter how conservative their governments might have been, had insisted on being at the forefront in military development, demanding, for example, that their armies be equipped with the most advanced artillery and projectiles. Yet because the military leaders who found these modern weapons in their hands did not understand the economic system which provided them, they were unable to understand the realities of employing these weapons in modern war. They had no notion whatsoever of the carloads of artillery projectiles that could be produced to support the war effort, nor did they really understand that this capability could become a part of their solution to military problems. Failing to appreciate the appetites of modern war before the war began, they were unprepared to fight it once it was underway. Thus the cry went up on both sides for more cannons and more shells within days after the German attack.

Yet even this heightened appreciation of the power of the modern weapons systems was insufficient for the demands of modern war. Trotsky recalled that at the same time that more artillery was needed the employment of barbed wire to protect the trench lines had given birth to equally strident demands for barbed wire. Even more critical was the need for wire clippers to cut lanes through the enemy's wire so that decisive offensive warfare could continue. "And we were treated to the spectacle, in the century of aviation, of an entire nation seeking scissors so it could crawl forward on its knees", Trotsky wrote. Eventually someone noticed that artillery shells could be fired at the wire to cut it, and at that point Trotsky detected the beginning of the imaginative use of artillery as a real machine of war, replacing the labor of men so that more could be accomplished with available resources. This seemed to be an indication of the sort of technological breakthrough that could develop during the war.[49]

Trotsky believed that the really decisive innovations would occur during the war rather than be the products of pre-war thinking. In his view,

> The military art appears in one respect to be the most revolutionary factor in history but in another respect it is the most conservative. The last argument of historical statism is material force, and in the clash of military organizations the level of technical, social, and political development of nations is displayed. That is why by means of militarism more than by any other new ideas, methods, and approaches gain governmental approval. But on the other hand, military ideas and principles appear to be crucial as well as unwieldy and expensive to implement. When they are implemented they become rifles, cannons, battleships, and fortresses – imposing objects which cannot be done away with easily. Thus it is necessary for them to be tested in real war if they are to be correct in their material manifestations.[50]

The necessary conditions for change could be found only when a war was actually being fought.

> It is necessary to examine in action the collision of living matter, not on the firing range, not on maneuvers where everything is controlled as if it were a stage, but in battle. War is necessary to improve war and to perfect methods.[51]

Trotsky was arguing that military techniques evolved slowly in response to specific needs, just as new processes were developed

85

and adopted in industry. Systems such as cannons or rifles seemed to change each other: first one underwent an improvement and then the other was improved in response.[52]

But in addition to these opportunities for evolutionary change which resulted from the exigencies of the battlefield, there seemed to be hope for a revolutionary change once war began. With the employment of modern mass armies, Trotsky noticed that "those who in peacetime found their vocation in the laboratory are now at war. How will their expertise change it? This is the hope for change – not the professional soldier".[53] Given these individuals who had the skills necessary to devise truly innovative breakthroughs, the only problem remaining was to find a place for their talents to be applied. Trotsky was confident that such weak points existed on the technological front. "Somewhere there is a monstrous gap in the technical apparatus of war",[54] he wrote, and he went on to discuss the possibility of overcoming the vulnerability of the internal combustion engine to devise a "colossal war machine which can move forward through the barbed wire".[55] Only when such a breakthrough occurred could a strategy of victory be developed. The military stalemate simply would continue at the strategic level until one side gained the technological advantage.

Even though Trotsky was accurately predicting the introduction of the tank, which did in fact have some influence on the termination of the war, he was overly pessimistic about the chances of a rapid breakthrough. He feared that the technological gap would be similar to the physical gap the generals were seeking: it would be easier to plug than to exploit.[56] In addition, he had no confidence in the armies' abilities to adopt changes rapidly. He wrote that "the technological combinations achieved at the end of one war become the technical framework for the model used in laboratory work in preparation for the next war". As a result, he feared that it would take "about ten years after the initial clash before the techniques of war are understood",[57] and he offered no real hope for an end to the strategic stalemate.

Historical hindsight gives us no real grounds to revise Trotsky's assessments. Technological innovation did provide hope for strategic advantage before the war ended, with the tank and the airplane heading most lists of devices which had already displayed their potential for changing the nature of warfare before World War I ended. Some military theorists (Liddell Hart, J.F.C. Fuller, Douhet, and Mitchell) understood the new techniques of warfare before Trotsky's ten year deadline had passed, but no military establishment had the necessary acumen to adopt wholeheartedly their theories within the decade. The lack of such commitment was not only a function of the irreversibility of military force structuring which Trotsky had discerned. Rather it resulted from the perception that victory had been achieved through a dramatic tipping of the military balance in favor of the Allies. American entry into the war, together with the successful naval blockade of the Central Powers, enhanced the Allied posture in the war of attrition and determined the outgrowth of the war in the absence of any real breakthroughs in the narrow strategic sense.

TACTICAL PROBLEMS

As Trotsky surveyed the strategic stalemate on all fronts in August of 1915 he wrote that the situation was "a mechanical manifestation of the historical blind alley into which the capitalistic world has driven itself".[58] The most obvious feature of this blind alley was the trench warfare which had made battle brutally expensive in its human costs even though decisive results could not be achieved. The tactics of trench warfare clearly dominated the military scene, and in his accounts of the war, Trotsky constantly strove to describe and analyse those tactics. By conducting numerous interviews with veterans and by reading the current military theorists he was able to develop a sound understanding of the tactical considerations involved in the war and he was even willing to extrapolate from contemporary military events in an attempt to predict the nature of tactics to be used in future wars.

Trotsky was convinced that the terrors of the World War's battlefields did not spell the end to war. In his view military science merely responded to the temper of the times, and with the World War having developed so many new possibilities for future experimentation he had no doubt that future generations would be plagued by military theorists who were ready to offer their governments solutions to the military problems encountered in the last war — solutions which would in fact be the products of lessons learned in the war.[59] Therefore an understanding of the tactical practices of the World War battlefield was essential if the future derivatives were to be properly appreciated. Setting these considerations before his readers, Trotsky proceeded to analyse the tactics of the trenches in some detail.

Trotsky's discussion of World War tactics is still valuable because he saw them as a complete break from nineteenth century tactics. In his analysis of the 1905 revolution he had revealed his knowledge of the fact that the machine gun and the modern artillery piece made it impossible for soldiers to mass in the open. Now he went one step further and began to analyse the significance of this change.

> In the old days of beautiful attacks across more or less open fields, one sight of the lines of riflemen, numerous but united into coordinated bodies, with a reserve following them prepared to reinforce when the onslaught began, was enough to frighten the already shaken enemy with the prospect of the coming impact. He could not know how it would end. He might abandon his position when the advancing troops were still one hundred meters away, having recognized the inevitability of defeat.[60]

Under those conditions the attacking force had the advantage because the dramatic nature of its physical momentum assisted in overcoming the defender. But in modern warfare exposure meant destruction – any soldier who could be seen could be killed. Now the man who stood behind a mass of earth and timber felt secure, capable of coping with the attacker's threat. In this situation the static momentum or inertia of the defender was superior.[61] Because the technology of modern weapons systems had been the factor which had swung the balance to favor the defender, there seemed to be little reason to expect that the advantage could be returned to the attacker. This could occur only if new weapons were developed which would once again allow the attacker to flaunt his power by attacking in mass formations in spite of the defender's firepower. In the meantime, the entrenched defender could hold his ground and suppress the attackers.

In his recognition of the superiority of the defense over the offense, Trotsky once again addressed psychological problems while analysing a situation that was ordinarily discussed in simple technological terms. The soldiers' feelings were just as important as the technological realities, for if soldiers were unwilling to stand and fight their weapons could not be effective. But with the advent of more deadly weapons, standing and fighting became easier psychologically as well as technologically. This helped to explain the front line soldier's preoccupation with improving his defensive position as a means of freeing his mind from the terror of his situation, but it also reflected the fact that the labor invested in the trench paid real dividends in neutralizing the enemy's fire, keeping the defending troop unit reasonably intact so that it could withstand the attack. Technology had contributed to a situation that gave the soldier in a defensive position every advantage.

Yet at the same time technology had changed the physical

properties of a defensible position. Before the war the key to defensive operations had been the fortress – a strong point with formidable walls of reinforced concrete studded with artillery pieces positioned to provide protection from attacks coming from any direction. But these elaborate fortresses had failed to stop the invading German army, and Trotsky accurately reported that "faith in fortresses fell when they fell".[62] This led him to ask what role would be played by fortresses in future warfare, and in order to answer this question he chose to analyse the nature of trench warfare as well. The resulting essay, "Fortresses or Trenches?", reveals his mastery of tactical principles in their broadest application as well as in the peculiar context of the situation of World War I on the Western Front.

Realizing that fortresses were thought to be outmoded, Trotsky set out to address the question of their future worth in a rational fashion. If one was to know whether fortresses were still needed, it was first necessary to know their purpose, and Trotsky detected two fundamental purposes.

> The principles of fortresses are derived from the obvious necessity to oppose the enemy in certain areas through which he must move, thus blocking his freedom of maneuver (examples of this type of fortress are seen at Toul, Brest Litovsk, and Peremysl), or to secure the main body of one's own army against enemy attack while it is concentrating (fortresses of this type are found at Liège and Namur).[63]

Since those considerations would continue to be preoccupations of the military planner, Trotsky rapidly concluded that strong permanent positions could not become outmoded. Conflicts of the future would be characterized by the employment of mass armies manned by citizen-soldiers who would have to be mobilized, and fortresses "follow from the 'nature of things' in mass conflicts".[64] Therefore the question became not whether or not there would be fortresses, but rather what form they would assume.

Trotsky recognized that it was merely fortresses which had been destroyed when the war began, not the military considerations which had led to their construction. Principles of construction might need to be changed, but the underlying principles of war which had prompted the construction were unchallenged. As Trotsky wrote: "The duel between heavy artillery and concrete has ended in a decisive victory for the artillery".[65]

The half-century before the First World War had witnessed numerous developments in artillery technology which made this outcome inevitable: the rifled cannon had greater accuracy; the breech-loader could be fired more rapidly; new explosives not only added to the effective charges which sent the artillery shells to the target but also allowed the manufacture of shells packed with explosive charges designed to have a tremendous destructive effect which far surpassed the weight of the projectile. At the same time improved techniques in machining and metallurgy made the application of all of these developments a rather simple matter. The concurrent improvement of field communications through the military adoption of the telephone meant that the increased ranges of the improved weapons could be used to engage targets beyond the sight of the gunners.[66] As a result a fortress which had undergone little change since Vauban's day had little chance of survival. The fortress of the future would have to be build to different specifications if it were to serve its intended function.

Recognizing that construction was the key to the problem, Trotsky looked to trench warfare to provide clues to the nature of future construction. This was quite natural, for the trenches appeared to be specialized fortresses which had been adopted by both sides:

> All operations on the Western Front have the character of fortress or siege warfare. True, it can be said that trenches, as a method of improvised mobile fortifications have brought an end to permanent fortresses, but such a statement would be rash. The French Front itself clearly shows us that future trenches, even though improvised, will never be "mobile": in an entire year they have not allowed either army to make a deep penetration. Here before us is a system of fortification which was not needed before heavy artillery.[67]

In delineating the elements which composed this new system of fortification Trotsky developed a complete analysis of the nature of trench warfare.

Identifying the elements which composed the trench system was a simple matter: "A trench is a ditch protected in the front by entanglements of wire and covered from both sides by machine guns".[68] Trotsky recognized the fact that the trench itself was only one element in the new type of warfare. The "ditch", with its supporting bunkers, provided the best possible protection from the new artillery. It was a difficult target to destroy, and its occupants could survive to withstand infantry assaults. The barbed wire and machine guns worked together to make this resistance possible. The wire slowed the enemy's assault and channeled it toward areas which could be raked by machine gun fire. The rapid-fire weapons could then destroy the attacking force before it could seize the defensive positions.

Modern artillery might have been considered a part of this defensive system since it was used routinely to supplement the suppressive fire of the machine guns. While Trotsky was aware of this use of artillery, he chose to argue that artillery was not a fundamental factor in the defensive system which would provide the model for the fortresses of the future.[69] His approach was reasonable. He recognized that

> The new artillery challenges the principles of fortresses from two sides: it not only makes it possible to reduce a fortress to a pile of rubble in a few days if not a few hours, but it also requires the stockpiling of enormous stores of artillery ammunition within the fortress. Even one of the new style, cut off from the centers of the country, must expend its military stores not over a period of months, as had been possible earlier, but in a siege of weeks if not days. This is one of the most powerful arguments of those who see no value in prepared fortresses.[70]

To counter this argument, Trotsky analysed the defensive uses of artillery in trench warfare. This led to the discovery that there were actually only two types of targets to be engaged: attacking troop formations or their supporting artillery pieces. The troops could be engaged effectively by machine guns, and the enemy artillery would not need to be neutralized if the trench system was properly constructed. Therefore, Trotsky could conclude that artillery actually played a secondary role in the defense and the problem of ammunition supply was not insurmountable.[71]

Having analysed the elements of trench warfare to derive the elements which would dictate the nature of the fortresses of the future, Trotsky combined those elements so that he could describe those fortresses:

> Around essential strategic points there will be several concentric lines of narrow trenches connecting them to a central web of barbed wire. The trench lines will be strengthened by using the most advanced construction techniques. They will contain easily shifted artillery batteries placed underground. Reliable shelters, storehouses, workshops, and large electrical generating plants will also be built underground. All of this will be dispersed over a wide area, so that heavy artillery will have no attractive targets. Such a fortress of the future, without

91

medieval forts, will be able to fulfill the functions fortresses ought to fulfill.[72]

While this analysis of the future of defensive warfare seems to herald the French post-war strategy that fostered the construction of the Maginot Line, Trotsky did not ascribe such sweeping application to a system which had been derived from simple tactical principles. He recognized the fact that this new type of fortress only reflected changes in construction techniques and did not modify the principles of war. He concluded his essay with a jibe at the "poor, scrofulous pacifist" who hoped to eliminate the possibility of another war by reinforcing the boundaries of states with continuous trenches.[73]

Effective fortresses could be built to withstand the existing weapons systems, but they were only a response to current technology. Rather than offering an end to war, they guaranteed that the old principles could again be employed in campaigns of the future.

Throughout this analysis of the future of fortresses Trotsky had kept sight of contemporary tactical principles. He recognized the primacy of defense resulting from existing weapons technology, and he accurately assessed the feeling of security the defender could gain from the earthworks that protected him. The defender's advantage did not seem to be threatened by any immediate revolutionary breakthrough in tactical methods, so the future seemed to promise little change. Given this view, Trotsky's insistence that the war would have to end before the revolutionary situation could develop becomes easier to understand. Neither action by the aroused masses nor military leadership by a specially trained revolutionary elite offered appealing odds for success when the realities of the military power equation so clearly favored the defender. In any revolution the forces of order would have the modern weapons, and the revolutionary forces would be attacking to gain the victory. The outcome seemed inevitable since even a few defenders could withstand massive attacks. The only real hope lay in allowing the war to run its course so that the forces of repression would be driven to the point of exhaustion in their war of attrition. At the same time work should proceed to weaken the resolve of the soldiers actually holding the modern weapons. While Trotsky did not share Lenin's defeatist slogans he agreed on the importance of propaganda work within the armed forces and looked forward to the day when armed might would not block the path to revolution.

CHAPTER SIX

The Military and the Revolution February–June, 1917

When revolution came to Russia Trotsky was in New York. He had been ejected from France in 1916 and then was detained briefly in Spain before sailing to the United States. His stay in this last place of exile was short, and Trotsky had reasonably fond memories of his days in New York when he wrote his memoirs. As a respected spokesman of the socialist movement he was met by Russian émigrés in New York City and immediately joined the editorial staff of the radical Russian-language newspaper, *Novyi Mir* ("New World"). He continued to comment on the war in Europe, a subject of increasing interest to readers in the United States in the early days of 1917. His oratorical skills combined with his insight into current problems to make him a popular speaker at labor organization meetings, and he was settling into the familiar life style of the émigré intellectual when news of the February Revolution reached New York.[1]

Initial reports were sketchy and some time was required to decide upon and make arrangements for the long-awaited return to Russia. During the two weeks before his March 27th departure, Trotsky addressed the significance of Russia's revolutionary events in the columns of *Novyi Mir*. Writing on 16 March, he evoked the image of "hungry mothers of starving children" whose curses directed at the established order had been the revolutionary tocsin for the workers of Petrograd. These workers had been the real strength of the revolution, for "the general strike traumatized the vital functions of the capital, paralyzed the power of the government, and trapped the tsar in one of his gilded dens". But an equally important factor had been the response of the army. "The soldier of the Petrograd garrison and the near-by units of the Russian army responded to the call of the revolutionary masses and made possible the first major victory of the people".[2]

Analysing the implications for the future from these events Trotsky asserted that the workers of Russia were in the process of

93

"liquidating not only the tsar but the war as well". But he sounded a cautionary note, compensating for his lack of first-hand experience in contemporary revolutionary events by drawing on the bitter experience of 1905 to write: "The revolutionary army – that will be the decisive stage in the development of the revolution".[3]

A few days later Trotsky returned to the critical relationship between the army and the revolution in additional columns for *Novyi Mir*. On 20 March he addressed the possibility that Russia would leave the war. He recognized the hope being expressed in liberal circles that revolutionary enthusiasm following the fall of a corrupt and inept regime would give the war effort in Russia new life. But he rejected this hope even though he predicted that this would be precisely the course of action attempted by the Russian bourgeois political element. This course of action was doomed to ultimate failure because it never could become an expression of the will of the masses. In the revolutionary environment they could not be fooled into continuing a war which simply did not pursue their class interests.[4]

In his next column on 21 March Trotsky investigated the practical considerations which made the breakdown of the war effort inevitable. The fact that the war brought workers and peasants together was most important, for this would allow the "unified proletarian cadre" in the army to deal with "peasant denseness". Trotsky outlined the type of revolutionary exchange he expected to occur between worker and peasant, and he predicted the consequences of success.

> "The landlord's estate, not Constantinople!" says the soldier-worker to the soldier-peasant, making it clear to him for what and for whom he is fighting the imperialistic war. And the success of our agitation and struggle against the war – first among the workers and then among the masses of peasants and soldiers – will determine how fast the liberal-imperialistic government will be replaced by a Revolutionary Workers' Government.[5]

The revolutionary path seemed clear. How quickly it could be traversed remained to be seen.

The first steps down that path were different ones for Trotsky. He had few problems gaining permission to return to Russia, but a few days after leaving New York harbor the Norwegian ship upon which Trotsky had booked passage docked at Halifax. The Russian passengers were subjected to detailed questioning by the British authorities, and on 3 April Trotsky, his family, and five other passengers were taken from the ship. Trotsky was taken to Amherst, a camp for German prisoners, most of whom were captured crewmen from German warships. Trotsky protested against his treatment, but nearly a month passed before intercessions on his behalf by the Provisional Government gained his release. The remainder of the trip to Russia was uneventful, and Trotsky arrived in Petrograd on 4 May.[6]

MILITARY CONDITIONS IN REVOLUTIONARY PETROGRAD

Trotsky later described the situation in Petrograd in those days as "a whirlpool in which men and events swept by me as swiftly as litter on a rushing stream",[7] and he soon was fully immersed in the torrent of activity that characterized the revolutionary capital. He had no real political organization. Lenin had returned to Russia a month earlier and tightened the reins on his faction of the Social Democratic Party. In doing so he had gained the support of many of the anti-war internationalists who might have been drawn toward Trotsky's wartime arguments. Trotsky could expect little success in his old role as party unifier, for the polarization of the Party on the issue of the war had been further exacerbated by Lenin's April Theses. Lenin's intransigent attitude toward Social Democrats who sought accommodation with bourgeois democracy made domestic issues a source of antagonism within the Party. Trotsky's small group of followers, the *Mezhraionka* (Inter-Borough Organization), did not form a genuine party. They were revolutionary intellectuals who opposed the war and the Provisional Government but continued to express suspicion of the centralistic Bolshevik methods. There was little separating their attitude toward issues from that of Lenin, and the Bolsheviks had the political organization necessary to gain mass support. Under these circumstances it is not surprising that the support Trotsky grasped in the whirlpool of revolutionary events was Lenin's.

The union of the *Mezhraionka* faction with the Bolsheviks was not formalized until later in the summer, but the unity of thought between Lenin and Trotsky was clear as soon as Trotsky addressed the Petrograd Soviet. In his first speech on 5 May he advocated the transferral of all power to the Soviets as the first step toward the formation of a truly revolutionary republic. Advocating this course of action while continuing to denounce the war put Trotsky in Lenin's camp. Revolutionary events made him one of Lenin's principal colleagues.[8]

When viewed at close hand the situation which faced the revolutionaries in Petrograd was not as clear as it had appeared from New York. One of the major areas in which confusion reigned was in the relationship between the revolution and the army. However, in writing for *Novyi Mir* in those first days after the revolution Trotsky had used the phrase "the soldiers of the Petrograd garrison and the nearby units of the Russian army", and the distinction drawn in that phrase was important.

Change was occurring throughout the Russian army, but since the army was not a monolithic institution, change differed with place and function. For the Petrograd revolutionaries the two most critical elements of the army were the Petrograd garrison and the soldiers and sailors occupying the defenses around the city. Since both the revolution's leadership and its staunchest support were centered in Petrograd, the survival of the revolution was dependent upon freedom of action within the city. That freedom could be obtained if the garrison and the Petrograd defenders remained favorably disposed toward the revolution, but it would never be guaranteed until sufficient armed strength was actively loyal to the revolution and willing to defend it against attacks from the rest of the army. Trotsky perceived this need and became a principal agent of the changes needed to gain that support. The war and the first cycle of revolutionary events had made the local elements of the army potential allies of the revolution. Trotsky set out to guarantee the alliance.

The garrison was an extremely complex institution even before the February Revolution, and the post-revolutionary changes which Trotsky saw when he entered Petrograd in May had made it virtually indescribable. He recalled:

> The soldiers sang revolutionary songs as they marched and sported red ribbons in their tunics. It all seemed as incredible as a dream. The tram-cars were full of soldiers. Military training was still going on in the wider streets. Riflemen would squat to charge, run a distance in a line, and then squat again. War, the gigantic monster, was still standing behind the revolution, throwing its shadow upon it. But the masses no longer believed in the war, and it seemed as if the training was going on only because no one had thought of stopping it.[9]

Throughout the war units which had been stationed in St. Petersburg before hostilities erupted had maintained reserve organizations in the city. This was necessary since the Russian military system required each regiment to maintain its own replacement system. The regiment was given a quota of recruits to train and these new soldiers replaced the unit's casualties. Regiments conducted training programs in all major cities where garrisons had been maintained before the war since these were the sites of the necessary barracks and administrative offices.

According to the military theory of the day Petrograd was an especially desirable training base because it had a wealth of barracks space and was well-located. Since it was the capital it had a good transportation net for the collection of recruits and good communications with the front allowing timely dispatch of replacement levies. Hospitals and doctors were more numerous in Petrograd than elsewhere in Russia, and this too increased the city's significance as a military center. Large numbers of sick and wounded soldiers were evacuated to Petrograd and then were attached to garrison units to convalesce. All of these factors combined to encourage the War Ministry to assign numerous newly-formed regiments to Petrograd during the course of the war, further inflating the size of the garrison. By February 1917 the garrison was composed of nearly fifty units and numbered more than 150,000 men. It could hardly be considered a fighting organization.

> The average stay of a soldier in the Petrograd garrison was six to eight weeks. The question of leave was a permanent irritant; inactivity and boredom in over-crowded barracks impelled the men to seek permission to go into town while the officers were chiefly concerned to have them confined to barracks because of the difficulty of keeping a check on them once they were caught up in the turbid waters of Petrograd life. Some of the companies were as many as fifteen hundred strong; there were new recruits – very young boys, who had not yet taken the oath of allegiance to the colours and the Emperor; yet others had already seen service in the field and spent long periods in hospital due to wounds or illness; these were bored and spoiled by the lack of discipline in the hospitals. There were a number of Petrograd intellectuals amongst them, as well as soldiers working in ordnance factories, and through these a certain amount of seditious propaganda reached the ranks.[10]

The lack of cohesiveness and low level of fighting skill which characterized the Petrograd garrison had been an important factor determining the outcome of the February Revolution. There is evidence that the Petrograd authorities perceived the possibility of riots and had developed plans to meet this contingency before the February crisis. But the plans were of little historical consequence since memoirists are virtually unanimous in noting the lack of coordinated effort to support detachments loyal to the government. Even the plans for feeding security patrols were inadequate.[11] The garrison lapsed into inactivity, passively accepting the outcome of the February revolution but becoming fertile ground for Bolshevik agitators.

The clear anti-war stand taken in Bolshevik propaganda was especially appealing in the Petrograd barracks since the men being trained there knew they were going to the front. But if the war ended there would be no front, and the terrors it held, which could be described so vividly by the veterans conducting training, would claim no more victims. To the soldiers of the garrison anti-war sentiment was more than intellectual posturing – it was a matter of personal survival.

Soldiers and sailors serving in the defensive works around Petrograd shared this concern even though their conditions of service were different. True fortresses such as Helsingfors and Kronstadt had not been converted into training garrisons. Three years of war at sea had been just as indecisive as war on land, and the German Navy retained its capability to mass forces against the Baltic coast or against Petrograd itself. The fortresses and the Russian Baltic Fleet were maintained to guard against this possibility. As the ice melted in the Gulf of Finland in the spring of 1917 the threat would increase once again, and the soldiers and sailors were vulnerable to anti-war arguments.[12]

The fortresses and fleet had been subjected to repeated levies for men and equipment throughout the war years, and as long as the war continued the military men of 1917 were subject to being sent down that same fatal path. Staying where they were was safer, but the duty was odious. The levies had left shortages of equipment, rations, and trained personnel. Wartime service required conditions of increased readiness. It was the age-old problem of doing more with less. This meant long hours, exhausting drills, poor food, and few leaves of absence. In the absence of a threat that could be clearly perceived by the common soldier or sailor this debilitating routine seemed unnecessary. When riots broke out in Petrograd the soldiers and sailors destroyed their tormentors. In the garrison authority had been tenuous and it dissolved in the face of conflict. In the fleet and fortresses officers were killed or driven off in a series of mutinies. When the new regime promised to continue the war the mutineers were in the forefront of the movement to change policy, and they developed an understandable affinity for Bolshevik propaganda.[13]

The garrison and fleet elements at Kronstadt were especially insistent in their demands for rapid changes following the February Revolution. On 16 May, less than two weeks after Trotsky returned to Russia, they declared: "The sole power in the city of Kronstadt is the Soviet of Workers' and Soldiers' Deputies".[14] This was in keeping with the course of action Trotsky had advocated in his first speech to the Petrograd Soviet, but the leadership there still rejected the seizure of power as an acceptable alternative. Mensheviks and Social Revolutionaries (SR) formed the majority, and they were committed to the existing *dvoevlastie* ("dual power") which left the legitimate right to rule in the hands of the Provisional Government while the Soviets served as guardians of working class interests. This majority denounced the slogan "All power to the Soviets!" as adventurism of the Left, arguing that large segments of the population would withdraw their support of the revolution if control passed to the Soviets. Disastrous reaction would follow.[15]

TROTSKY'S APPEALS TO THE MILITARY

Trotsky rejected this interpretation. In a speech to the Petrograd Soviet on 26 May he defended the Kronstadt resolutions, asserting that they anticipated the end of *dvoevlastie* and reflected the path the revolution must select if it was to be safe against counter-revolutionary forces.[16] The next day he made the ferry trip to Kronstadt and completed his identification with the workers, soldiers, and sailors there when he said, "We, Kronstadters, will stay at our post on the left flank of the great army of the Russian Revolution".[17] Trotsky won the support of Kronstadt, and he did not lose it throughout the revolutionary period. The Kronstadters were rough and unruly, but, for the reasons outlined above, far more capable of armed action than the Petrograd garrison. Trotsky now had an armed ally far more formidable than any he had had in 1905.

Throughout June Trotsky worked to maintain the support of the Kronstadters while making arguments which appealed to the garrison. On 2 June he charged Kerensky with attempting to break up the revolutionary regiments of the garrison and exterminate the Kronstadters so that a counter-revolutionary uprising could succeed in Petrograd.[18] Since the political theme did not necessarily motivate the soldiers in his audience, he also condemned the class nature of the war. Kerensky would decimate the garrison regiments by levying troops for the front,[19] where they would spill their blood for no good reason. This single action would continue the war and weaken the revolution.[20]

On 9 June Trotsky addressed the problem of the war in a speech to the All-Russian Congress of Soviets. Through careful development of his themes he was able to appeal to delegates from military units without using the usual arguments calling for the dissolution of the army. Instead, he referred to the Russian army as part of the revolutionary process and then proceeded to analyse the army as if it were already on the side of the revolution.[21]

Trotsky began by pointing out that the literature which denounced "anarchy in the army" was being written by defensists and patriots. True revolutionaries recognized that "this is our army, that heroic army which achieved the Russian Revolution".[22] They also knew that the army could not possibly stand in the forefront of revolutionary socialist consciousness since it embodied the entire society.

> This is an army which emerged from Russia's social and political conditions with all their backwardness, with all their anachronisms; it has not yet fully overcome barbarism. ... Everyone understands that problems of self-interest and personal consideration still remain strong in the army and demoralize it.[23]

But Trotsky insisted that to dwell upon these problems was incorrect, for every military detachment also contained individuals who were willing to share the risks of revolution, and these progressive elements were the factor which made the army a part of the revolution. What appeared to be anarchism in the eyes of patriots and defensists was in fact self-sacrifice and heroism when considered from the point of view of the revolution.

> To the good fortune of all Russian history our revolution destroyed forever the psychology of locusts and cockroaches ... where 100,000 died passively, spontaneously, not thinking of their sacrifice and not facing the question of the subjective or objective purpose of this sacrifice. I say, Damn that historical period; we have left it behind! If we expect heroism now it will not be mass, elemental, unthinking heroism but the heroism which comes from each individual consciousness.[24]

Trotsky then went on to embrace the notion of a democratized army, denouncing as bourgeois Philistines those who argued that democratic reforms could not be applied in the army until a successful offensive had satisfied the nation's war aims.

> I maintain that the army of the great French Revolution, by voting or other suitable means, was able to decide and did

100

decide on an offensive with complete rationality. Why isn't this done? All actions indicate there are no such unifying purposes for the army in our times. ... If there were there would be no complaints of demoralization, disunity, and anarchy.[25]

Trotsky asserted that the lack of genuine democratic support for the war should not upset the revolutionaries for they recognized that "the army has dragged the war on its back from the days of the old autocratic regime".[26] The soldiers' unwillingness to shed blood for a cause they did not support simply meant that the war would have to end or repressive measures within the army would be needed on an unprecedented scale. The revolutionaries could see which alternative was preferable. Their army must leave the war if its revolutionary potential was to be retained.

This theme was developed more fully in Trotsky's "Theses on the War" which he published in *Vpered* ("Forward") on 28 June. Having denounced the class nature of the war and the material and spiritual irrationality of those who argued in favor of renewed offensive action, Trotsky concluded by outlining a proper approach toward the war which would "re-establish close ties between the army and the population". Essentially he called for the immediate solution of Russia's internal problem through transfer of power to the Soviets, admission of political weakness, negotiation of a separate peace, and general recognition of the aspirations of the masses.[27]

Within six weeks after his return to Russia Trotsky had made genuine progress in gaining military supporters. His consistent anti-war stand gave him an initial advantage which he was able to exploit by avoiding any temptation to become anti-military. He actively courted the masses in the army, recognizing their contributions in the first phases of the revolution and urging them to prepare for more sacrifices in the name of revolutionary progress. His attitude encouraged action by the more radical elements in the army, and he hoped this would move entire units into the revolution's camp.

Writing in his *History of the Russian Revolution* long after the event, Trotsky developed his theories of the relationship between the army and the revolution in 1917. These later theories fit the speeches and articles he had prepared in May and June of that year. He had denounced outmoded notions of discipline in the army, and in his treatise on the revolution he noted that

The revolutionary soldiers – sympathetic, wavering or antagonistic – are all tied together by a compulsory discipline whose threads are held, up to the last moment, in the officer's fist. The

101

soldiers are told off daily into first and second files, but how are they to be divided into rebellious and obedient?[28]

Such division could occur only when events sparked action, and even then soldiers would be reluctant to act in support of the revolution unless they had some assurance that their actions would lead to revolutionary victory. Failure meant discovery and return to the barracks under the old discipline for punishment at the hands of reactionary elements. In 1917 it had been essential for leaders such as Trotsky to support progressive acts by the military and to shield from retribution those soldiers who had taken action. The army could be won over for the revolution only if this was done. By late June the formula had been successful in and around Petrograd.

Trotsky was not the only leader responsible for this success. His position on military matters was generally in consonance with that of the Military Organization of the Bolshevik Party, and this gave him a genuine bond with a few key Bolshevik activists specializing in revolutionary affairs in the military.

TROTSKY AND THE MILITARY ORGANIZATION OF THE BOLSHEVIK PARTY

The need for specialized propaganda for use in the army had been recognized by the Bolshevik leadership within days after the February Revolution. On 2 March the Petrograd Bolshevik committee had decided to prepare special leaflets for distribution among the soldiers, and on 31 March the Party formed its Military Organization with N. I. Podvoisky as President.[29] The new Military Organization concentrated its efforts on units in and around Petrograd, working to gain the support necessary to overthrow the bourgeoisie and using the flow of peasant-soldiers through the units as a means of transmitting the Bolshevik propaganda message to the countryside.[30] Special newspapers addressing appropriate issues in simple and forceful language were published for the troops. The first of these, designed to reach the garrison, was *Soldatskaia Pravda* ("Soldiers' Truth"), which began publication on 15 April. By the end of April it had been joined by *Golos Pravdy* ("Voice of Truth") in Kronstadt, *Volna* ("The Wave") in Helsingfors, and *Okopnaia Pravda* ("Truth for the Trenches") to be distributed at the front. *Soldatskaia Pravda* was the foremost of these specialized papers, and by 15 June it was being published in editions of 400,000 copies.[31]

The Military Organization knew soldiers well enough to go beyond the publication of newspapers which were likely to be used as nothing more than field expedient cigarette papers or boot liners in the hands of semi-literate troops. Clubs were opened at appropriate points in Petrograd, and by late May many of the regiments had their own Party club rooms where issues and programs could be discussed.[32] Clubrooms allowed Party agitators to identify soldiers who were potential supporters and to develop their commitments to such a degree that they would seek Party membership.[33]

This emphasis on agitation at the grassroots level was the principal difference between the Bolshevik program in the army and the efforts of other parties. The other revolutionary parties had won early successes in gaining the right to represent the soldiers. Trotsky explained this phenomenon by arguing that

> The soldiers trustfully elected those who had been for the revolution against monarchist officers, and who knew how to say this out loud: these were volunteers, clerks, assistant-surgeons, young war-time officers from the intelligentsia, petty military officials – that is, the lowest layers of the *new middle caste*. All of them almost to the last man inscribed themselves, beginning in March, in the party of the Social Revolutionaries, which, with its intellectual formlessness perfectly expressed their intermediate social situation and their limited political outlook. The representatives of the garrison units thus turned out to be incomparably more moderate and bourgeois than the soldier masses. But the latter were not conscious of this difference: it would reveal itself to them only during the experience of the coming months.[34]

The clubs, the newspapers, and the continuing efforts of the Military Organization were all designed to help the soldiers interpret those experiences properly.

While the Bolsheviks were building support with the rank and file in the units the Mensheviks and SRs worked to maintain seats on soldiers' committees. They were successful, and in the first months of democratization of the army the Mensheviks and SRs looked much stronger than they actually were.[35] These parties concentrated on Front, Army, and Corps committees and their representatives had a good deal of visibility. But at the same time they were being coopted by events and had no real contact with the troops. By late June their connection with defensist and social patriotic themes had become unsatisfactory to the soldiers they were supposed to represent. The Bolsheviks concentrated their efforts within regiments, trying to win over entire companies, then battalions, and

103

finally the regiment itself. Using this approach they were successfully undermining the apparent strength of their opponents.

Trotsky was heavily involved in all of this activity, contributing
articles to *Soldatskaia Pravda* and making speeches at the soldiers'
clubs. In addition on 9 June he threw the support of his Inter-
Borough Organization behind the Bolshevik Military Organization's plan for a demonstration, and after the demonstration was
aborted he made a heated verbal attack on Tseretelli's effort to
disarm units that had gone over to the Bolsheviks.[36] The effort to
ensure revolutionary victory through action within the military
fitted Trotsky's theories and absorbed a large part of his energy
throughout the remaining months before the Bolshevik victory.

THE MILITIA

At the same time that elements of the army were being won over to
the revolution the masses were being prepared for armed action. In
this area, too, activity had begun before Trotsky returned to Russia.
One of the first casualties of the February Revolution had been the
Petrograd police. Many individual policemen had been killed or
disarmed, and the institution had been discredited both in the
eyes of the masses and in the plans of the authorities. The initial
decree of the Provisional Government which prohibited the re-
assignment of revolutionary military units from Petrograd also
provided for "replacement of the police by a people's militia with
an elected administration, subordinated to the organs of local self-
government".[37] The Petrograd Soviet cooperated with this initial
effort by the Provisional Government because

> The soldiers who were roaming the streets ransacking houses,
> setting fire to police stations and government buildings, and
> wasting ammunition shooting into the air could not be relied on
> to defend the revolution if dependable Tsarist troops were sent
> from the front. Some kind of cohesion and leadership ... was
> needed, and there was little time to lose.[38]

As militia organizations began forming it soon became obvious
that this aspect of revolutionary government was far more complicated than the initial decree had intimated. A modern Soviet scholar
identified the heart of the problem when he wrote, "Two concepts of
militia were current: the 'European democratic' and the 'class
oriented' ".[39] Both the Soviet leadership and the Provisional
Government were thinking of the "European democratic" model
when the decree was published, but many groups in Russia soon

thought of the militia as a class-oriented institution actively engaged in the struggle for power. This confusion over its role combined with the power vacuum accompanying its creation to make the workers' militia an extremely complex institution.

There were three main elements in the early militia organization: the city militia – units replacing the police in the maintenance of public order and under the control of the Provisional Government; the factory militia – units formed to protect the rights of workers and under the control of unions or factory organizations; and the party militia – fighting organizations formed by interest groups to protect members against depradations by armed groups whose disagreements with a given political program went beyond the provisions of Roberts' Rules of Order.[40]

It was this last group which contained members who were most actively "class-oriented" and devoted to the offensive use of militia force for political ends. The Left did not have a monopoly in this endeavor, but since elements of the Right had long been accustomed to police and military units performing this function for them they demonstrated neither the creativity nor the single-mindedness found in the parties of the Left. Anarchists, Bolsheviks, Mensheviks, and Social Revolutionaries all had their fighting organizations. Clubs, fists, an occasional pistol or saber, and a modicum of organization were enough to protect a meeting, guard a headquarters, or escort a leader.[41] More sophisticated militia capabilities were required if class interests were to be advanced.

The development of an improved militia was undertaken by the Petrograd Soviet in early March. A 7 March decision called for the formation of a worker's militia which was to be subordinated to the government militia. This move attempted to consolidate the three militia elements and reduce the potential for violence while guaranteeing the protection of workers' interests. The Mensheviks and SRs supported the initiative, but the Bolsheviks were less cooperative. Nonetheless a workers' militia was formed, and over half of the 20,000 members of the city militia were workers. This meant that the workers' sections of the city were guarded by the workers' own militia and any party gaining support of this organization would have tremendous freedom of action.[42]

The Bolsheviks were engaged in gaining that support. On 3 March the Central Committee of the Bolshevik Party had decided to organize a military-militia commission charged with the responsibility to form proletarian militia cadres. Aleksandr Gavrilovich Shliapnikov was selected to undertake the task of arming and organizing the workers.[43]

Both aspects of the assignment were difficult. In those first days after the February Revolution most of the weapons in the hands of the workers' militia were "trophies" of encounters with the police and garrison units during the Revolution. There was no system for supplying additional weapons, and the Soviet had no authority to issue arms from governmental stores. Party militia leaders developed a partial solution to the arms shortage by bringing weapons under organizational control, associating them with militia units rather than with individuals. This made maximum use of available weapons since they could be passed on with a guard post in the 24-hour security mission which was the characteristic function of the first militia units. It also reduced "hooliganism" since a significant number of weapons were given up by individuals.[44] However, this administrative control measure did not supply sufficient weapons to meet the needs of the units, and weapons shortages continued to limit the potential of the workers' militia throughout the summer.

On the surface, organizational improvements would seem easier than arming the workers since no material support was required. However, overcoming the workers' suspicion proved to be a problem nearly as intractable as finding a source of arms. Initial militia organization had been spontaneous, and while the resulting units might have been loosely knit, devoid of military skills, and poorly armed, their members saw themselves as filling a vital role. Their missions seem to have been narrowly utilitarian – for example, "Keep our factory open!" "Defend the print-shop workers!" "Keep hooligans out of our street!"[45] – rather than being broadly class-oriented as the Bolsheviks expected. These utilitarian missions resulted in units having complex loyalties with little relationship to party membership, and many militia members were openly hostile to party organizers since these seemed to be engaged in efforts to coopt the militia units for new, less desirable purposes. By early April most units had declared their subordination to the will of the appropriate district Soviet, but they were still suspicious that they would become auxiliaries to party fighting organizations if they gave free rein to party activists.[46]

By mid-April the continuing lack of coordination and overlap of functions within the militia structure caused the Petrograd City Duma to form a temporary commission to recommend improvements. Rostov, who was a member of this commission, drew up a detailed program for the organization of "Red Guards", and on 28 April a leaflet proclaiming the formation of the Red Guard was distributed in the workers' districts.[47]

Thus when Trotsky returned to Russia the Red Guards had been recognized as a part of the revolutionary environment even though their formations were still weak and poorly organized. The majority of the Executive Committee of the Soviet still questioned the necessity for their existence, but they could not be disbanded. Trotsky immediately took the side of the Red Guard, arguing that the revolution could not triumph unless the workers were armed and organized. In the aftermath of the attempted 10 June demonstration Tseretelli renewed the efforts to disarm the workers' militia, recognizing the fact that increasing radicalism was making it a challenge to the Soviet leadership rather than a support. Trotsky denounced Tseretelli's proposal, not only on the grounds that it would leave the workers vulnerable to counter-revolutionary violence, but with the threat that "the working class has never in its history given up without a struggle the weapons which it has received from the hands of the revolution".[48] The moderate leadership of the Soviet faced a dilemma: attempting to disarm the workers would lead to bloodshed; allowing militia efforts to continue under growing Bolshevik influence could also end in violence. The latter alternative was scarcely more appealing than the former, but the Bolshevik response to Soviet discipline on 10 June had been reassuring, and the Red Guards continued their drills unmolested.

CHAPTER SEVEN

Trotsky and the Organization of the Petrograd Revolution

THE JULY DAYS

The first real test of the revolutionary potential of the Petrograd garrison and militia came on 3 July. A massive armed demonstration by soldiers and workers resulted in scattered violent conflict, but when the crisis passed on 5 July power remained in the hands of the Provisional Government and the moderate leaders in the Soviet. Trotsky later characterized this event as "an extensive reconnoiter", in which

> We had to make a retreat, under onerous conditions. The party, to the extent that it was preparing for the insurrection and the seizure of power, considered – as did Lenin – that the July Demonstration was only an episode in which we had to pay dearly for an exploration of our own strength and that of the enemy, but which could not alter the main line of activity.[1]

Trotsky was not able to view the flow of history so calmly at the time. He had not personally dealt with the security or military aspects of the demonstration – these had been the concern of the Bolshevik Military Organization.[2] However, he had been heavily involved in developing the conditions precipitating the demonstration, and he shared the Bolshevik goal of staying at the forefront of mass revolutionary action. Throughout June he continued to advocate an immediate end to the war, assumption of all power by the Soviets, and the conduct of a victorious revolution which would set off a revolutionary chain of events throughout the world.[3] On the eve of the July Demonstration he spoke at an emotion-charged meeting of the First Machine Gun Regiment. This unit was the key element in the July Demonstration. It was quartered in the Viborg District, which was a stronghold of the radical revolutionary factions, and had been heavily influenced by propaganda designed to bring garrison units over to the revolution. Revolutionary tendencies were enhanced by necessity – the regiment had just received a levy sending nearly two thirds of its strength to the Front, and desperate measures seemed to be justified. Trotsky was one of several anti-government speakers who received a warm welcome from a crowd of nearly 5,000. Trotsky's virtuosity as an orator, together with his usual themes of "End the War", and "All Power to the Soviets", contributed to the will for action. By the time he left the meeting the First Machine Gun Regiment was committed.[4]

Trotsky's next stop was the *Narodnyi Dom* ("House of the People"), a gathering place for workers and soldiers where he was a well-known and welcome speaker. Anti-government sentiment was running high on 2 July, and Trotsky's comments advocating the transfer of all power to the Soviets resulted in an enthusiastic clamor.[5]

When the demonstration actually began on 3 July Trotsky was with the Workers' Section of the Petrograd Soviet in the Tauride Palace. He later asserted that the demonstration came as a complete surprise to him,[6] and he may have been working to prevent an armed demonstration.[7] But there is no direct evidence of Trotsky's position on the specific issue of armed demonstration in the critical hours before the units formed to march. His program required mass action. He continued to advocate those programs in his public appearances to already-inflamed groups on the day before the demonstration, so it is difficult to accept the conjectural assertion that he opposed active measures at the last moment. Since he spoke to garrison units he would have known that they insisted on bearing arms in any demonstration. Yet it is important to recall his commitment to the notion of "Soviet legality" which drove him to seek majority support in the Soviet to lend legitimacy to mass action.[8] In the absence of such support he may have hoped to forestall a premature mass action, but work within the Workers' Section of the Soviet would not seem to be the proper effort to achieve this result.

When the demonstration erupted his attempts to reduce the level of violence and maintain control could not be mistaken. He shuttled back and forth between the demonstrators and the embattled Soviet, at one point dramatically rescuing Chernov, the SR Minister of Agriculture, from a lynch mob.[9]

The Soviet was not swayed by the demonstration and made no move to seize power from the government. Ultimately its members were saved by the arrival of loyal detachments from the reserve battalions of the Izmailovsk, Semenovsk, and Preobrazhensk Regiments.[10] In the heat of the moment many observers thought that the relief detachment had come from the front, but it was in fact a portion of the garrison. Its loyalty to the Provisional Government demonstrated the need for further revolutionary effort in the garrison, but the failure of the demonstration threw obstacles in the path of that work.

As the workers and soldiers returned to their homes and barracks with nothing to show for their efforts but the wounds received in brushes with loyal troop detachments, a far-reaching program to discredit the Bolsheviks was gaining momentum. On 5 July Petrograd newspapers carried charges that Lenin and his party were receiving German funds and acting as agents of the German government.[11] The Provisional Government quickly blamed offensive failures at the front on the disloyalty and unrest in the capital. Loyal troops destroyed the *Pravda* printing presses, and the Provisional Government issued warrants for the arrest of key Bolshevik leaders, charging them with having organized the demonstration on 3 and 4 July.[12]

Trotsky's name was not included in the list of those to be arrested. His return to Russia had not taken him across Germany, and he had not yet formally joined the Bolshevik Party, so the label "German Agent" did not fit Trotsky so well. He immediately grasped at this distinction as a means of publicizing his interpretation of the July Days.

On 9 July Trotsky wrote in *Vpered* that he shared the Bolshevik program. However, he stressed his belief that the demonstrations were the result of objective realities, not the work of agitators. In Trotsky's interpretation of events the Bolsheviks and Mezhraionka group "rejected the politics of Pilate" and provided leadership and organization for the demonstrations in spite of the risks of counterrevolutionary provocation. Provocation occurred and blood flowed, but only the left wing elements were being charged with contributing to the violence. This indicated to Trotsky that the Bolsheviks were being used as political scapegoats and that power should pass to the revolution to prevent injustice.[13] On the following day he published an open letter asking why he was not arrested along with the Bolshevik leadership since he was equally "responsible".[14]

Two weeks passed before Trotsky was arrested, and during that time he defended Bolshevik actions and challenged the moderate leadership of the Soviet. In discussing the significance of the July Days in speeches before the Soviet he challenged the notion that the demonstration was an armed uprising.

> An armed uprising by armed people must have a goal which these people are trying to accomplish. What was their goal? The Tauride Palace was totally unarmed. The arming of the

masses was unrelated to the taking of some sort of strategic positions or political centers. Considering this we see that there was no armed uprising. This was an elemental demonstration which included counter-revolutionary elements.[15]

This was a compelling response to the charges of conspiracy to gain control of the government. The demonstrators had ample weaponry, yet they had not used force to impose their will on the leaders of the Soviet. Trotsky recalled the distinction he had made in 1905: masses could die for the revolution or organized groups could fight for it.[16] He argued that the July demonstrators fell into the first category. They had not been organized to seize power, and they made no direct attempt to do so. Critics asked why the garrison troops, sailors and militiamen had armed themselves if they had no plans to use force. Trotsky replied: "The masses took arms because they knew of counter-revolutionary activities. We agree with you that this was a mistake".[17]

Liberals and moderate socialists did not accept Trotsky's interpretation of the July Days as an elemental phenomenon which erupted in spite of the efforts of the Bolsheviks. On 23 July Trotsky was arrested and sent to the Kresty Prison where he had awaited trial in 1905. The prison was crowded and living conditions were poor. But as Isaac Deutscher noted,

> With such debaters as Kamanev, Lunacharsky, Antonov-Ovseenko, and Krylenko, political debate flourished. Among the inmates were also Dybenko and Raskolnikov, the leaders of Kronstadt. Here were assembled nearly all the chief actors of the October insurrection and nearly the whole first Bolshevik Commissariat of War.[18]

Cell block debates have no stenographic record, so it is impossible to reconstruct the intellectual exchanges which occurred within the Kresty's walls in July and August. The debaters plunged into a whirlwind of activity when they were released, and the weeks in prison faded into insignificance in the following years that turned debaters into memoirists. However, the fragments of evidence that exist support the assertion that during these weeks in prison Trotsky rejected spontaneous mass action and recognized the inevitable need for control of armed force in making the revolution.

When he entered prison Trotsky may have been opposed to the continuation of the Party Military Organization in spite of the failure of spontaneity in the July Days.[19] If this was the case his conversion during the six weeks in prison was dramatically complete. When he left prison on 4 September he immediately began to work with the Committee for Struggle against Counter-Revolution, which was the forerunner of the Military Revolutionary Committee.[20] The intellectual forces operating on Trotsky while he was in prison were sufficient to cause such a change, for the inmates included party activists who had worked at the front as well as politically conscious soldiers and sailors.[21] These, together with Bolshevik leaders who had been directing the party efforts within the military, provided convincing evidence of the potential for organized action. Events occurring outside the prison's walls also contributed to Trotsky's growing commitment to the use of organized force.

THE KORNILOVSHCHINA

As suppression of the Bolsheviks continued into August, forces seeking a government capable of conducting a successful war effort became stronger. Kerensky became Prime Minister of a new coalition cabinet on 24 July, and his policies reflected a dramatic departure from the programs of the moderate socialists. Thousands of soldiers were sent to the front in spite of earlier promises to keep the garrison intact.[22] This was a military necessity if the war was to continue, but it gave each front-line organization a new contingent of unwilling troops who had been the recipients of heavy doses of anti-war propaganda. Generals chafed under the conditions of poor discipline and lack of support which they saw as the explanation for continuing military failures. When Kornilov was appointed commander-in-chief on 31 July he demanded that the death sentence, which had just been reintroduced at the front, be reinstated in the rear as well.[23] Throughout the following weeks he made additional demands unacceptable to the leadership of the Soviet but appealing to Rightist elements. The situation became complicated when Kerensky realized that Kornilov's aims threatened his own authority as well as that of the Soviet. As Kornilov's regiments approached the capital Kerensky turned to the Left for support.

Even though Bolshevik activities had been sharply curtailed after the July Days the armed forces responsive to their party program had remained large. Some elements of the garrison had been sent to the front, but the thousands of recruits and veterans who stayed in the capital were still responsive to the Bolshevik "End the War" appeal. To maintain a semblance of discipline and order the government had forbidden Bolshevik propaganda activity in the barracks, but off-duty soldiers could still attend meetings, and the party press continued to produce special newspapers for the military audience.[24] The Party Military Organization continued to operate, concentrating its attention on the garrison units rather than Red Guard activities.[25]

The workers' militia also had been suppressed after the July Days, but the factory militia actually grew.[26] Local security at factories was needed under all circumstances, and this defensive nature of the factory militia made it a less formidable political force.[27] The factory militiamen performed their duties on the job, protecting the factory during their work shift. Soviet scholars have shown that many individuals who were drilling as members of the Red Guards on weekends and after work were members of the factory militia at their job sites.[28] As a result reduction in workers' militia activities was not a fatal blow to the militia movement. Weapons were in short supply, so expansion of the movement would have had little meaning. During July and early August the militia organizations maintained their organizational cohesion but languished. The call for assistance to meet the Kornilov threat brought a dramatic change.

The government opened its arsenals to the arms-hungry militia organizations. Bonch-Bruevich later cited this as the decisive factor in forming the Red Guard.[29] The magnitude of the change can be seen in the Viborg District where the Red Guard received 940 rifles to supplement the 270 that had been available before the Kornilovshchina.[30] At the same time Bolshevik organizers were given free run of the barracks and the militia headquarters. The influence of the Bolshevik Military Organization soared, and after the threat from Kornilov's forces had been neutralized the stage was set for active organization of armed force in support of the revolution. The Left had acted responsibly in defeating Kornilov, and the Committee for the Struggle against Counter-Revolution formed for the contingency offered the perfect vehicle for further action by the time Trotsky joined it. Prison walls had prevented his direct participation in the organization of the defense against Kornilov, but he had not been totally without influence. His newspaper articles had denounced Kerensky's promise to use "blood and iron against anarchism from the left and counter-revolution from the right". Trotsky argued that this was a workable formula against the Right where class enemies could be clearly identified, but it could not work against the Left where the masses of the population were involved. Given this governmental attitude he asserted the need to organize the workers, in the streets and at the front, to protect them against the counter-revolutionary attitudes of the government.[31]

Trotsky had also influenced events themselves when a delegation of Kronstadt sailors came to his prison cell to receive guidance. They had been asked to assist the government in defending Petrograd against Kornilov, and they hesitated to act, seeing Kerensky's government as having few claims to their loyalty. Trotsky urged them to show their sense of responsibility to the revolution by participating in the defense effort.[32] When the counter-revolutionary threat had passed Trotsky was free to organize workers and soldiers for the seizure of power which would give them a genuine defense against counter-revolution.

PREPARING THE ARMED FORCES FOR REVOLUTIONARY VICTORY

The first steps in the preparatory process were not particularly dramatic. Trotsky returned to his familiar themes: end the war; pass all power to the Soviets. In the uncertain days of September these slogans were even more inflammatory than they had been in July. The war was going very poorly. The Germans had mounted a counter-offensive after Kerensky's offensive failed in early July. Most of Eastern Galicia fell into German hands in late July and early August, and Riga fell on 21 August.[33] By September continuing German gains began to threaten the approaches to Petrograd.

During these difficult days Trotsky published a pamphlet entitled, "When Will the Accursed War End?"[34] He wrote that in Berlin people were saying, "We can't stop now, we're winning", while in Petrograd the defensists were crying, "We can't stop until we have halted the Germans. We must be patriots before we can think of peace". Since the army had continued to erode and the masses showed no interest in the continuation of the war, he proposed that the slogan *Voina do kontsa* ("War to the end") be replaced by *Konets voine* ("End to the War"). Since the Provisional Government still insisted on the continuation of the war in spite of public attitudes Trotsky concluded that power would more properly be vested in the Soviet.

Far more power had passed to the Soviet in the aftermath of Kornilov's abortive coup. Rifles were only a simple physical manifestation of the increased power of the workers. The new committees for the defense of the revolution were as reluctant to surrender their newly-won power as the workers were to give up the arms they had been issued. Throughout September Kerensky attempted to disband the "self-appointed committees" which were undermining the authority of the government. At the same time he tried to regain control in the army and navy by dissolving the special armed detachments of soldiers and sailors which had been formed to guard the revolution. The Soviet resisted these efforts and denounced them in an *Izvestiia* editorial on 6 September.[35] The Left was guarding its enhanced power jealously.

For the Bolshevik Military Organization the changed situation after the Kornilovshchina offered new opportunities for organization and training of loyal elements. Increased support within the garrison regiments, together with more arms in the hands of workers, meant that training programs for the Red Guards could begin in earnest. Working through district soviets and local Party organizations the Military Organization sent instructors to the militia units to teach basic military skills which would put the enthusiastic workers on the path to becoming effective fighting units.[36] At the same time this assignment of instructors to the militia units gave the Bolshevik Military Organization ideal contacts with the militiamen. The instructors were accepted as sources of military–technical knowledge, and they could impart political training at the appropriate moment. They could also gauge the military effectiveness and political reliability of the various units on a daily basis.

Military effectiveness was still largely a function of weapons availability, but the training programs, where effectively conducted, held considerable promise. Instruction included drill, manual of arms, tactics (skirmishing, street fighting, barricade defense, and trench warfare), techniques of security while moving and in position, maintenance of weapons and equipment, and dry firing drills.[37]

Improvements in organization were also contributing to greater effectiveness. In the Viborg District, which appears to have had the most advanced organization, squads of ten men were gathered into platoons of 40–60, with the size of the platoon depending on the local situation. Two platoons formed a company; four companies were a battalion; two battalions were a regiment. The primary staff for directing activities was at the district level, but on 13 September the commanders of the Petrograd militia resolved to form a directive organization for the entire Red Guard composed of five representatives of the militia and one each from the Central Executive Committee of the Petrograd Soviet, the central factory-mill committee, the central union committee, the inter-district council, and the city duma.[38] The central organization appears to

115

have had little effect, but the Kornilovshchina and the growing German threat to the capital had given credence to the notion of centralized control. This was an important factor in Trotsky's mastery of the military forces in Petrograd.

On 20 September the need for armed workers was questioned at the abortive Democratic Conference.[39] Trotsky answered that they were needed

> First, to provide a real bulwark against counter-revolution, against a new, more powerful Kornilovshchina. And second, if a genuine dictatorship of revolutionary democracy is to be established and this new power offers a true peace which is rejected, then I tell you in the name of our party and through it for the proletarian masses, that the armed workers of Petrograd and all Russia will defend the revolutionary cause against the forces of imperialism with such heroism as is unknown in all of Russian history.[40]

While the first of these defensive functions was nothing new, the second postulated a new domestic power relationship and a new role for armed force. "If a genuine dictatorship of revolutionary democracy is to be established" – these words connoted the transfer of all power to the Soviets. The use for the militia which followed was unlike any that had been contemplated in the past. Instead of protecting their factories and neighborhoods against saboteurs and hooligans, instead of protecting their revolutionary bastions against domestic counter-revolutionaries, the armed workers would now defend against the forces of imperialism.

This new task required greater concentration of effort than had been needed in the past. The Bolsheviks, in Trotsky's declaration to the Democratic Conference, demanded universal arming of the workers and expanded Red Guard organization. They also turned their attention to the army, advocating complete freedom of agitation at the front and a completely democratic organization in the army.[41]

Trotsky gave additional emphasis to the army's role in his initial speeches in the Soviet after becoming President of that body on 25 September. Recalling the role of the Izmailovsky Regiment in arresting the 1905 Soviet, he noted that "the Izmailovsky Regiment of those days and of today are entirely different. We feel that we are much stronger now than we were then". He also asserted that this changed relationship with the army could be maintained only if the Soviet avoided identification with the reactionary class interests of the Provisional Government: "[The seizure of power by the Soviet] is necessary so that every honest Russian soldier knows that the honest people's power has placed in our hands all resources of the country and they are being distributed without deception and with no toleration of looting".[42]

These references to the army and its relationship to the Soviet indicate Trotsky's desire to gain control of a fighting army rather than to neutralize the army's counter-revolutionary potential by destroying its fighting power. By late September the Russian army was virtually exhausted, and Left propaganda had contributed to its weakness. Yet as the locus of power shifted to favor the Left within the Soviet and as Trotsky gained control in the Soviet he did not reject the possibility of using regular forces alongside militia in the defense of the revolution. The regular forces might be unimpressive on the battlefield, but the militia units were not particularly formidable. Gaining the support of regular units would augment the numerical strength of the revolution and it would add technical capabilities (especially field artillery and engineer) which were in short supply in the militia's preponderantly infantry forces.

Early evidence of Trotsky's desire to establish Soviet control over a viable army can be seen in a resolution which he drafted for the Petrograd Soviet, promulgated on 11 September. The resolution first reviewed the efforts of the Provisional Government to maintain control of the army and to shore up its reactionary element so that it would continue to serve as an agent of repression. It then analysed the aftermath of the Kornilov movement in this context, noting that a dangerous backlash of retribution against officers had occurred even though many military men of all ranks shared the goals of the revolution. Lynchings and assassinations were denounced as "not the proper methods for a revolutionary purification and restoration of the army". Soldiers were encouraged instead to "strengthen your organization, stand in defense of the revolution, and demand and facilitate the beginnings of a democratic army".[43]

As the September days passed the need for a new army became apparent as the German threat to Petrograd grew. The front lines advanced toward the capital throughout September. On 4 October the Provisional Government secretly discussed moving the government out of the city. Rumors of this discussion spread rapidly, and on 6 October Trotsky made an impassioned speech in the Soldiers' Section of the Petrograd Soviet against abandoning the revolutionary capital. As a result of this speech the Soldiers' Section passed a resolution supporting his position.[44] On 8 October

Rodzianko's speech on the possibility of surrendering Petrograd was published,[45] and Trotsky's earlier overtures to the military took on a new dimension.

Trotsky developed a new theme in his speeches, evoking the image of Petrograd as the revolutionary equivalent of the evangelist's "city on a hill" which served as a beacon to the exploited who still suffered in darkness. Defense then was defined in terms of revolutionary gains, not territorial considerations. The most critical revolutionary asset, to be defended at all cost, was Petrograd. In addressing the Congress of Soviets of the Northern Region he reviewed the development of the "revolutionary front" within the army which would meet this defensive requirement. The first glimmer of its existence had been perceived in the April Crisis. It had grown stronger in June and emerged fully in the July Days, which were a spontaneous manifestation of the democratic, revolutionary expectations of the army. The revolutionary front received its complete expression (and first victory) in the defeat of Kornilov. "When Kornilov rose up the revolutionary army did not renounce Kerensky but improved the revolutionary front and gave Kornilov a heroic rebuff ... The only power which can [deal with the Kornilovists and liquidate the war] is the power which is effective in the army, i.e., the power of the Soviets".[46] Meanwhile Trotsky was actively supporting the formation of a Military Revolutionary Committee to formalize this power of the Soviet in the army.

The need for a special committee of the Soviet to deal with the defense of the revolution resulted from the Provisional Government's attempt to move nearly one third of the garrison to the front. The Army issued orders for such a move on 9 October, and within hours the Soviet was debating the significance of the proposed move. Similar orders had preceded Kornilov's move on the capital in August, so the counter-revolutionary implications of the order could not be ignored.

But the objective situation was not the same in October. In August the German forces had just seized Riga. Now they stood virtually at the gates of Petrograd. Was the Provisional Government proposing a militarily correct defensive measure in moving garrison units to the nearby front? Would additional troops solve the problems of defense at the front and thus save Petrograd? How could additional troops be the answer when the regime had never used them effectively in the past? Wasn't the Provisional Government preparing to abandon Petrograd, and shouldn't its order to the garrison be seen as an attempt to destroy the forces of revolution while insuring its own survival? The Soviet could not answer the technical military questions in its meeting of 9 October, but it felt sure it must guard against counter-revolutionary plots. It adopted a resolution authorizing the Executive Committee to organize a committee for revolutionary defense which would collect information concerning the defense of Petrograd and its approaches to determine technically correct defensive dispositions. It would also take measures to arm the workers to assist in the defense against the attack which the Right seemed to be plotting.[47]

The Executive Committee appointed Lazimir, an SR, as the chairman of a group to translate the resolution into a specific organizational charter. This work was completed rapidly, as the situation demanded, and on 11 October the Executive Committee accepted its product:

> The immediate tasks of the revolutionary staff for the defense of Petrograd are:
>
> 1. To determine the minimum armed force and supporting material and supplies necessary for the defense of Petrograd, and to prevent their removal.
> 2. To accurately account for and register the individuals who compose the garrison and its stocks of food and equipment.
> 3. To develop a working plan for the defense of Petrograd.
> 4. To develop measures to protect Petrograd against pogroms and desertions.
> 5. To bolster revolutionary discipline among the workers and soldiers of Petrograd.
>
> The revolutionary staff will be divided into the following sections to perform its duties:
>
> (1) Defense, (2) Supply, (3) Liaison, (4) Workers' Militia, (5) Information Bureau, (6) Message center, (7) Headquarters.[48]

The new committee would give the Soviet the necessary capabilities to master the problems of the "revolutionary front" to evaluate the military–technical as well as the political aspects of proposals generated by the Provisional Government and Army Headquarters. This implied a new level of dual power, for now the Soviet had become directly involved in the routine details of military affairs.

DEVELOPING THE TACTICS FOR THE SEIZURE OF POWER

While the Soviet was organizing to deal with the threat against the revolution the Bolsheviks were discussing the insurrectionary tactics required to gain control of the revolution. Since early September Lenin had been advocating an armed insurrection by forces loyal to the Party. Opportunity for decisive action seemed to be slipping away with each passing day, yet he could not convince the Central Committee of the need for action. Finally the same threat to Petrograd which prompted action in the Soviet gained majority support for Lenin's position. After a late-night meeting on 10–11 October the Central Committee declared that an armed uprising was inevitable and the time was ripe.[49] On 11 October both Party and Soviet took the decisive step toward organizing the armed forces of the revolution.

Trotsky saw no reason to jeopardize the Party's move toward power by separating it from actions already approved by the Soviet. His reflections on 1905 had led him to the conclusion that a non-factional agency was required to gain support of the masses in an insurrectionary situation. The Soviet had the opportunity to form the necessary agency in its Military Revolutionary Committee. On 12 October he urged the Soviet to form a committee that was "not a museum piece but a practical organization, having its own organizational strength, formed of three factions – Bolsheviks, Mensheviks, [word illegible – probably Left SRs]".[50] This composition would allay fears that the Committee was nothing but a means for the Bolsheviks to seize power, and this was important if the Soviet was to address the very real problem of defending Petrograd.[51] On 16 October the Soviet approved the formation of the Military Revolutionary Committee with Left SRs and Anarchists joining the Bolsheviks who composed the majority of its membership.[52]

On the same day, the Executive Committee of the Soviet, having received accounts of continuing difficulties in the militia, decided that formal statement of the mission of the Red Guards would enhance their capability as a defensive force. The Committee declared that the Red Guards were an organization of armed force of the proletariat for the struggle with counter-revolution; all organizational activities and the political direction of the Red Guards were now a function of the Soviet, under the Military Revolutionary Committee.[53]

The Military Revolutionary Committee went to work immediately. It established contact with the commissars of the general staff of the Army of the Northern Front, the staffs of the Petrograd and Finland military regions, and the staff of the Baltic Fleet. By 21 October the Military Revolutionary Committee was sending commissars to the units of the Petrograd garrison and was collecting statements of military readiness from the Red Guard units.[54]

Throughout the period of initial organization the Military Revolutionary Committee was ignoring the growing conflict between its activities and the authority of the Provisional Government. On 19 October Trotsky had openly called for transfer of complete power to the Soviet, arguing that this was the best way to defend Petrograd against the German threat. The new leadership, reflecting the will of the people, could declare an immediate armistice signalling the end to the war.[55] The Government had grown increasingly suspicious of Bolshevik intentions and had put its plan for security of the city into effect on 20 October. There was no overt clash, but both sides were on guard. The next evening the Military Revolutionary Committee informed the staff of the Petrograd Military Region that the garrison had recognized the Committee's authority and the staff should now do the same. The staff refused, and there were no grounds for negotiation. On the morning of 22 October all garrison units were notified that the staff had broken with the revolution and the Military Revolutionary Committee had assumed control of the garrison.[56]

EXECUTING THE PLAN

Translating this declaration into genuine control still required careful work. To reduce the chance of an attack from outside the city Trotsky reassured the soldiers at the front that the efforts to preserve the garrison were not designed to deprive the front-line troops of support. Instead, the workers and soldiers of Petrograd were guaranteeing the survival of the revolution in spite of the efforts of reactionary generals. By organizing the defense of Petrograd under direction of the Soviet, the Military Revolutionary Committee was ensuring the defeat of the bourgeois elements who were in fact the reason that soldiers were still in the trenches.[57]

Within Petrograd the efforts to gain actual control continued on 23 and 24 October. On the authority of the Soviet arms and ammunition were issued to the Red Guard.[58] Commissars continued to do their work within the garrison. By the night of 23–24 October Antonov-Ovseenko reported to the Soviet that the Military Revolutionary Committee had gained the allegiance of the garrison.[59] On 24 October the Military Revolutionary Committee published a list of 51 garrison units with telephone numbers citizens could call if they encountered counter-revolutionary activity. Help would be sent immediately. The degree of success achieved can be seen in the units on the list. It included such bastions of Junker reaction as the Nikolaevskii Cavalry School and the Mikhailovskii Artillery School.[60]

Barracks telephones must have been busy on 24 October, for early that morning Kerensky called loyal troops into Petrograd from the suburbs. The Bolshevik print plant was ransacked at 5.30 a.m., and by 11 a.m. the Military Revolutionary Committee had notified garrison units to stand by for orders. Throughout the afternoon and evening minor skirmishes were fought around drawbridges controlling communications into the city. During the night of 24–25 October Red Guards and garrison detachments took control of critical points. By the morning of the 25th it was obvious to Kerensky that he had lost control of the armed forces available in the city. He departed for the front to rally loyal units against the insurrection. The Military Revolutionary Committee consolidated its position during the day, receiving formal endorsement of its actions from the Soviet by mid-afternoon.

During the night of 25–26 October the Winter Palace was taken, leaving only minor pockets of resistance in Petrograd. However, on the morning of 26 October Kerensky started back toward Petrograd with Krasnov and his cossacks. The real test of the revolution's defensive strength was about to begin.

Trotsky began preparing for this threat almost as soon as Soviet authority had been declared. On 26 October *Rabochii put'* carried his appeal:

> The people's revolutionary army must not allow the dispatch of unreliable military detachments to Petrograd from the front. Act through words and persuasion, but where this does not suffice prevent their departure by ruthless application of force.[61]

On 29 October, after Kerensky had failed in his efforts to raise the Gatchina garrison in his support, Trotsky was exultant. Kerensky's failure meant that he would have only cossack cavalry, and without infantry his force would be less formidable.[62] This was important because the force available to defend the revolution was hardly awe-inspiring. The fighting capabilities of the Red Guards were virtually untested, and the militia had not been trained for field operations. The garrison was passive and badly weakened by a lack of leaders since most of the officers were not trusted. The ability to move and support a force was ensured by the cooperation of the railway workers and the Red Guard auxiliary, but battlefield performance was difficult to predict.[63]

Before Kerensky's forces had made sufficient headway to actually threaten the capital an uprising of Junkers erupted in the city. Centered primarily in the Engineering School, which was located in a fortress near the Plain of Mars, the Junker uprising threatened to become an internal distraction limiting the forces available to fight Kerensky. Detachments of Red Guards and sailors surrounded the Junker schools and attempted to send in negotiators. These were fired upon, so armored cars and artillery were added to the investing forces. The attackers issued an ultimatum, and when it was ignored the artillery opened fire. The Junkers surrendered, and the advantages of controlling sufficient armed force became apparent to the revolutionaries.[64]

When their forces clashed with those of Kerensky and Krasnov on the following day at Pulkovo, the outcome was not so certain. Trotsky later recalled a picture of mass confusion with too few officers and a serious shortage of technical knowledge. Artillery was brought into place to bolster the courage of the raw troops and to deter the cossack cavalry. However, guns, limbers, and caissons had to be brought together by men who had little knowledge of their tasks, and there was a "great deal of fumbling". The effort paid off, though, for the artillery inflicted some casualties, the cossacks' commitment evaporated, and the revolution was safely defended.[65]

The successful defense of Petrograd as a revolutionary headquarters resulted from months of preparatory work. Trotsky had participated in virtually all stages of the effort, and the victory proved the validity of many of his ideas on the solution of military problems facing the revolution.

In seizing power the Bolsheviks had mobilized, trained and armed workers to fight for their cause. But they also gained the support of army units so that the forces resisting their move to power were weakened. Trotsky was in the forefront of this movement. His speeches swayed soldiers to the Bolsheviks' side and his newspaper articles supplied arguments for agitators at the front and in the fortresses. By both words and actions Trotsky had helped to build the insurrectionary power of the Bolshevik movement.

Trotsky had also provided an important smokescreen of legitimacy for insurrectionary activity. By linking the Petrograd Soviet to basic issues of military preparedness and by asserting the Soviet's responsibility to defend Petrograd against counter-revolutionary activity, Trotsky gave both Red Guards and garrison soldiers the necessary opportunity to prepare for overt military action. Even though the asserted legitimacy was specious, the Soviet's authority could be challenged only by direct armed action. Supporters of the Soviet would have been able to interpret this action as the counter-revolution Trotsky had prepared them to meet, and the outcome of the ensuing clash would have determined the question of legitimacy.

The clash was neither immediate nor direct. Under the guidance of the Military Revolutionary Committee the insurrectionary elements built their strength and were able to seize control of the capital. Their successful defense of the city against Kerensky's supporters gave them a significant base from which to expand their revolution, but many more battles had to be won before their position was secure.

CHAPTER EIGHT

Conclusions

After the October victory Trotsky served the new regime by negotiating peace with the Central Powers. Revolution did not sweep Europe during the negotiations, and the lack of further victories to expand the revolution meant diplomatic defeat. The treaty of Brest–Litovsk was a severe set-back for the Bolsheviks, but it allowed them to retain their revolutionary base. In the meantime anti-Bolshevik sentiment grew stronger in Russia and gained outside support. Still the European proletarian revolution did not materialize to save the Bolsheviks, and the stage was set for civil violence.

Trotsky's theories of insurrection had gained sufficient support of armed elements to put the Bolsheviks in power, but his broader political theories of worldwide revolution did not match reality. This put Trotsky in an anomalous situation. He became the military leader of a revolution limited to Russian soil and found himself defending that local revolution even though the world revolution did not materialize. In the course of defending the revolution he earned his reputation as a military theorist, but the lack of insurrectionary victories in other capitals paralleling that of the Bolsheviks in Petrograd meant that his battlefield victories in Russia could bring no more than tactical advantage.

In Trotsky's view strategic victory was ineluctably linked to world revolution. He understood modern warfare well enough to realize that if decisive victory was to be attained, battlefield skill had to be combined with enormous production capacity, transportation capability, and popular support. The Bolsheviks could hope to gain the last element in Russia, but the economic base of the old empire could not supply the other prerequisites for decisive military victory. Successful revolutionary movements in the industrialized countries were absolutely essential to the long-term survival of the revolution in Russia.

Trotsky led the military struggle for survival while the Bolsheviks awaited other revolutions that never materialized. Since this leadership situation resulted from a theoretical anomaly, Trotsky was

125

forced to improvise. He had studied military matters in the context of revolutionary victory – he was not prepared to direct the efforts of a conventional army in a prolonged struggle.

The leadership of the Red Army during the Civil War is a subject deserving careful study, but it is beyond the scope of this work. As Commissar of War Trotsky was a key figure, but an adequate analysis of the direction of the war effort must transcend the limits of biography. Even in 1917 the collective leadership of the Military Revolutionary Committee had become significant, and throughout the Civil War there were committees and staffs having collective responsibility exceeding that of any specific member. We might use Trotsky's interaction with these bodies as a vehicle to improve our understanding of the workings of the military leadership. However, current Soviet attitudes would make a researcher proposing such a methodology unwelcome. There may be grounds for revising the current Western view which gives Trotsky a predominant role in the direction of the Red Army's efforts, but access to archival materials in the Soviet Union would be a precondition to assuming a revisionist stance.

A review of the knowledge of military affairs which Trotsky had accumulated before 1918 reveals that he had the potential to earn the central role he enjoys in Western versions of the Civil War. Like many other Russian revolutionaries Trotsky was not particularly drawn to military affairs. Yet he recognized the importance of overcoming military resistance if the revolution was to be victorious. In analysing the defeat of 1905 Trotsky saw the need for armed elements loyal to the revolution, but he also perceived the requirement to reduce the effectiveness of the army opposing the revolution.

Neither of these endeavors offered fertile fields for revolutionary activity in the years of repression which followed 1905, but Trotsky improved his understanding of the problem by participating in Party debates. Larger issues of Party unity and the general political line captured most of his interest, but Trotsky continued to address the issue of armed violence. With pogroms and summary courts martial prevailing in Russia, Trotsky recognized the risk inherent in taking up arms prematurely, and he became increasingly critical of individualistic terrorism.

His observations during the Balkan Wars reinforced his view that individuals or guerrilla bands were peripheral to the main revolutionary effort. But at the same time the Balkan experience improved Trotsky's understanding of modern armies. He saw the troops mobilize and march off to battle. He watched the progress of their campaigns with genuine interest, and he began to understand war in human rather than in abstract terms. This made it no more attractive, but Trotsky could begin to appreciate factors motivating the men who fought, and he witnessed war's impact on them and on the societies from which they came. As he reported the war Trotsky became more familiar with military operations, and he demonstrated a growing interest in strategic and tactical problems.

These interests served Trotsky well when he reported on World War I. He became increasingly aware of the problems of modern warfare, and he began to understand the means revolutionaries should use to bring the army to the side of the revolution. He realized that the sacrifices of trench warfare bound officers and troops together and made them unique and apart from the rest of society. Yet these were men who were exploited by capitalist interests, and once they recognized the root cause of their misery they would join enlightened workers in making the revolution.

When Trotsky returned to Russia in 1917 he was able to apply this image to actual situations. Unlike many of his colleagues who were satisfied with a passive army, he fostered active participation by military units on the side of the revolution. These units were of doubtful military value, and their political motivation was even more uncertain. Yet they provided an invaluable complement to workers' militia units having better political credentials but inadequate military preparation.

Trotsky was ready for the military challenges of the revolutionary situation of 1917, and the victorious Bolsheviks owed much to his preparedness. Yet their victory was as much a result of circumstances Trotsky had not predicted as it was a result of his theoretical insights. Almost all of his thoughts on the insurrectionary action posited a strong and repressive state as the revolutionaries' adversary. By 1917 the opponent had been weakened and increased freedom of action made organization, agitation, and military preparation far easier than Trotsky had contemplated.

The Russian army was more badly weakened by the long war than Trotsky could have hoped. This made it easier to penetrate units and bring them over to the revolution. It also meant that there were few military units ready to charge the revolution's barricades, and those which charged did so with little vigor. But even in its weakened state the army did not succumb to revolutionary threats or promises as readily as Trotsky had predicted.

Even though his theories were not perfectly suited to objective circumstances in 1917 Trotsky had a clear image of what should be done to gain revolutionary victory. Even his most basic political tactics in October reflected an understanding of battlefield realities that military men can admire. By arguing for "Soviet legality" Trotsky was putting the insurrectionists on the strategic offensive so that they could achieve their goals while leaving them on the tactical defensive to reduce their risk. On the battlefield this is the essence of maneuver – placing elements so that they cannot be avoided but at the same time can destroy enemy forces seeking to dislodge them. Trotsky and the other members of the Military Revolutionary Committee used the tenuous legitimating authority of the Petrograd Soviet to put forces in position to defend Petrograd against counter-revolution. Having done so, they dramatically increased the odds for victory.

After studying war in the Balkans and Western Europe Trotsky knew the tactical advantages of the defensive: troops had better protection against the firepower of modern weapons, they were easier to lead since they did not need to be deployed under fire, and lack of training caused fewer serious difficulties because defensive troops were not called upon to respond to complex orders. He also understood that battle required technical skills. He sought soldiers and officers to train forces loyal to the revolution and to fight alongside those forces. This insight, which proved valuable in 1917, became one of the best-known characteristics of Trotsky's program as Commissar of War. By mobilizing sufficient numbers of soldiers and leaders with requisite technical skills he was able to build an army capable of offensive operations, for Trotsky had also learned that decisive victory can be attained only through offensive action.

When Trotsky became Commissar of War he also recognized that a sophisticated production capability had to exist alongside a well-developed training base if an adequate military force was to be fielded. The lessons of the Western Front were clear: the ability to bring industrial capacity to bear upon the battlefield was a key to victory in modern warfare.

The Bolsheviks were not able to muster overwhelming industrial capacity during the Civil War, and without that capacity or sympathetic revolutions abroad, there was no hope for strategic victory following the initial success in Petrograd. Trotsky's solution to the relationship between the military and the needs of the revolution was adequate for the seizure of power in Russia, but it lacked transcendent implications. The world revolution he had predicted did not follow, and the meaning of that initial victory was fundamentally altered. The Civil War, the debates over the proper defense establishment and strategy of the new Soviet state, and innumerable other military realities flowed from the unpredicted situation. Trotsky improvised solutions to many of these new problems, but these solutions were not directly dependent upon the considerations outlined in this study. We have seen that before 1917 Trotsky had studied military affairs in a revolutionary context and had developed original, workable ideas for using military power to gain political objectives. He was ready with a feasible approach to the military problems of revolution when opportunity presented itself in 1917.

Notes

CHAPTER ONE

1. "Military revolutionary theory" was not Trotsky's invention and he did not claim exclusive jurisdiction in the field. Marx and, to a greater degree, Engels had recognized the need to address military matters in the context of revolutionary affairs. The tradition remained strong in Russia through Trotsky's formative years.
2. Leon Trotsky, *Sochineniia*, 12 Vols. (Moscow, 1925–27).
3. The holdings of Russian-language newspapers in the New York Public Library's Slavic Collection were adequate for these tests of completeness and accuracy. I had satisfied myself on this point when an extremely valuable research tool appeared. See Louis Sinclair, *Leon Trotsky: A Bibliography* (Stanford: Hoover Institution Press, 1972).
4. Isaac Deutscher, *The Prophet Armed* (New York: Random House, 1965), pp.477–85.
5. Neil M. Heyman, "Leon Trotsky as a Military Thinker" (unpublished Ph.D. thesis, Stanford University, 1972).
6. Detailed biographies of Trotsky are readily available. The outline of his early years which follows is drawn from Leon Trotsky, *My Life* (New York: Pathfinder Press, 1970), pp.1–174; G.A. Ziv, *Trotskii: Kharakteristika po lichnym vospominaniam* (New York, 1921), pp.1–127; and Deutscher, *The Prophet Armed*, pp.1–144.

CHAPTER TWO

1. Leon Trotsky, *1905*, trans. by Anya Bostock (New York: Random House, 1971), p.296.
2. Ibid., p.384. The Bostock translation gives the date of "My Speech Before the Court" as 4 (17) October 1907. This error probably has been carried from the Russian text used for translation. The Russian second edition of *1905* recorded the date incorrectly as 1907, and this error was repeated in Part 2 of Vol. 2 of Trotsky's *Sochineniia*. That the correct date is in fact 4 October 1906 is beyond question. This translator's error is understandable, and fortunately it is virtually the only flaw in the work.
3. Ibid., pp.394–5.
4. Ibid., p.386.
5. Ibid.
6. Ibid., p.392.
7. Ibid., p.393.
8. Engels was fascinated by this question and wrote extensively on the subject. Trotsky's writings indicate a familiarity with much of this literature, but during this period he was most heavily influenced by Engels' Introduction to Marx's *The Class Struggle in France*, which inspired the rebuttal summarized here.
9. Trotsky, *1905*, pp.390–1.
10. Ibid., p.267.
11. Ibid., pp.269–70.
12. Ibid., p.266.
13. Ibid., p.268.
14. *Iskra* ("The Spark") was the official newspaper of the Russian Social Democratic Labor Party, but at this time it was under rather tight Menshevik control. In Isaac

Notes

Deutscher's words, Trotsky's willingness to be published there meant that "to outsiders Trotsky remained a Menshevik". Orientation within the Party had little impact upon questions of military organization in 1905, however. Isaac Deutscher, *The Prophet Armed*, (New York: Random House, 1965), pp.117–44, provides an excellent study of political considerations before and during the revolution. Retrospective interpretation of military events of the 1905 revolutionary experience later became a factor in party disputes. This problem is discussed in Chapter 3.

15. Leon Trotsky, *Sochineniia*, Vol. 2, Part 1: *Nasha pervaia revoliutsiia* (Moscow–Leningrad, 1925–27), pp.234–5.
16. Sidney Harcave, in *The Russian Revolution of 1905* (London: Collier–Macmillan Ltd., 1970), p.168, writes that "as late as October 3, Lenin, writing from Geneva to the fighting committee of the St. Petersburg Bolsheviks, upbraided them for the slowness of their preparations for an armed uprising. He pointed out that, though the committee had been talking for months about bombs, as yet it had not a single bomb".
17. Trotsky, *1905*, p.107.
18. Ibid., p.156.
19. Ibid., p.146.
20. This story is told in Chapter XI of Leon Trotsky, *My Life* (New York: Pathfinder, 1970), p.142.
21. Trotsky, *1905*, p.138.
22. After fifty days of existence the St. Petersburg Soviet was disbanded and its leaders were arrested on 3 (16) December.
23. Trotsky, *1905*, p.173.
24. Ibid., p.240.
25. Ibid., p.241.
26. Ibid., pp.246–7.
27. Ibid.
28. Ibid., p.241.
29. Ibid., p.398.
30. Ibid., p.396.
31. Ibid.
32. Harcave, *Revolution of 1905*, p.173. This proposal was not implemented.
33. "Soldaty russkoi armii i russkogo flota". Proclamation issued 14 June 1905. L. Trotsky, *Sochineniia*, Vol. 2, Part 1, pp.248–9.
34. Trotsky, *1905*, pp.177–8.
35. Ibid., pp.208–9.
36. Ibid.
37. Ibid., p.208. Trotsky's assessment of the revolutionary realities seems to be an accurate reflection of recruiting practices in the Russian Army of the late Imperial period. Literacy was demanded by the nature of the duties in artillery and engineer units, and most peasant recruits were not literate. Factory workers were more likely to be literate, and they were also accustomed to working with precision machinery similar to that found in an early twentieth century howitzer battery. Thus the needs of the service demanded the allocation of most ex-factory workers and most literate soldiers to these units. See John S. Curtiss, "The Peasant and the Army" in Wayne S. Vucinich, ed., *The Peasant in Nineteenth Century Russia* (Stanford: Stanford University Press, 1968), pp.108–32, and M. Semin, "Zhizn soldatov v tsarskoi armii" in *Krasnyi Arkhiv*, 98 (1940): 145–76.
38. Trotsky, *1905*, p.207.
39. Harcave, *Russian Revolution of 1905*, pp.220–1.
40. Trotsky, *1905*, p.258.
41. The Soviet's proposal and Witte's response were reported in *Izvestiia* on 20 Oct. 1905. See Trotsky, *Sochineniia*, Vol. 2, Part 1, pp.281–3.
42. Trotsky, *1905*, pp.258–9.
43. Strike figures are from Harcave, *Russian Revolution of 1905*, p.221.
44. Trotsky, *1905*, p.102.
45. Ibid., p.264.

46. Ibid., p.269.
47. Unit histories of loyal units which fought against revolutionaries and mutineers are scarce, but the memoir of V. Vladimirov, "Otriad leib-gvardii Semenovskogo polka v dekabr'skie dni na Moskovsko-Kazanskoi zh. d." in *Revoliutsiia i R.K.P. (b) v materialakh i dokumentakh* (Moscow, 1925), 3:437–54, gives an excellent insight into the phenomenon described here. The Semenovsky Guards regiment was a critical element in the suppression of the Moscow uprising. While the early Soviet archivists used this account to demonstrate the bravery of the workers who defied the regiment, the memoir dramatically points up the fact that this defiance hardened the resolve of the troops and commanders of the Semenovsk. The railway workers who used guerrilla tactics against the punitive expedition as it moved toward Moscow not only paid with their own lives, but apparently risked the lives of the Moscow revolutionaries as well. The regiment resented its casualties, hardships, and delays and arrived on the scene in Moscow fully prepared to carry out its bloody business of destroying the revolution. Of course this elite regiment was not typical of all those which remained loyal, but the fact that guerrilla tactics will make regular army units "fighting mad" seems to have been just as true in Trotsky's time as it is in our own.

CHAPTER THREE

1. Trotsky, *1905*, trans. by Anya Bostock (New York: Random House, 1971), pp.349–476.
2. Cf. N.M. Heyman, "Leon Trotsky as a Military Thinker", (unpublished Ph.D. thesis, Stanford University, 1972).
3. Isaac Deutscher, *The Prophet Armed* (New York: Random House, 1965), pp.175–86.
4. G.V. Plekhanov, in *Iskra* No. 20, 1 May 1902, republished in *Revoliutsiia i R.K.P. (b) v materialakh i documentakh* (Moscow, Gosizdat, 1925), 2:275 (hereafter as *Rev i RKP (b)*).
5. When SD agitational work within the army began late in 1901, the "Volia" group apparently enjoyed the greatest success. This probably can be explained by the fact that their program was designed to appeal to down-trodden elements from both the city and the countryside and thus fit the social composition of the army's ranks quite nicely. Of course the advocacy of terrorism would have great appeal within the army, since it promised the opportunity to destroy the oppressive military leadership when the revolutionary situation was at hand. The "Volia" group quite naturally concentrated on the army since it seemed to be an obstacle to the mass revolution and an excellent target for terrorism. See M.I. Akhun and V.A. Petrov, *Bol'sheviki i armiia v 1905–1917gg* (Leningrad, 1929), pp.9–12.
6. G.V. Plekhanov, "V nastoiashchee vremia terror ne tselesoobrazen", *Zaria*, Nos. 2–3, Dec. 1901, in *Rev i RKP (b)*, 2:263–4.
7. Ibid., pp.260–1.
8. G.V. Plekhanov, "O Demonstratsiiakh", *Iskra*, No. 20, 1 May 1902, in *Rev i RKP (b)*, 2:272.
9. Ibid., p.273.
10. G.V. Plekhanov, "Russkii rabochii klass i politseiskie rozgi", *Iskra*, No. 22 (July 1902), in *Rev i RKP (b)*, 2:265.
11. On Plekhanov's reaction to 1905, see Samuel H. Baron, *Plekhanov: The Father of Russian Marxism* (Stanford: Stanford University Press, 1963), pp.254–78.
12. Plekhanov, p.268.
13. V.I. Lenin, "Revoliutsionnaia armiia i revoliutsionnoe pravitel'stvo" in *V.I. Lenin o voine, armii i voennoi nauke*, 2 vols. (Moscow, 1958), 1:131 (hereafter as *Lenin o voine*).
14. Ibid., pp.129–30 (emphasis in the original).
15. Ibid., p.131.
16. V.I. Lenin, "Uroki moskovskogo vosstaniia" in *Lenin o voine*, 1:243–9.

17. Ibid., p.245.
18. Ibid., pp.245–6.
19. Ibid., p.247.
20. V.I. Lenin, "Chto delat'? Nabolevshie voprosu nasego dvizheniia" in *Lenin o voine*, 1:25.
21. The following analysis is based upon the text of the resolution "Vooruzhennoe vosstanie" in *Kommunisticheskaia partiia sovetskogo soiuza v rezoliutsiakh i resheniiakh s"ezdov, konferentsii i plenumov Tsk*, 8th ed. (Moscow, 1970), 1:152–3 (hereafter as *KPSS v rez*).
22. Here the Bolsheviks apparently referred to the disappointing November strike in St. Petersburg staged in sympathy for the Kronstadters (See page 21, above).
23. *KPSS v rez.*, 1:153.
24. The following analysis is based upon the text of the resolution, "O vooruzhenom vosstanii", *KPSS v rez.*, 1:175–6.
25. "Partisanskie boevye vystupleniia" in *KPSS v rez.*, 1:154.
26. Lenin expressed these views in his essay on the December Uprising, in which he stated his admiration for the courage demonstrated by the revolutionary crowds while admitting that lack of organization and inadequate technical proficiency had been primary factors in their defeat. See V.I. Lenin, "Uroki Moskovskogo vosstaniia", *Lenin o voine*, 1:246–7. The same assessment is found in memoirs of members of early Bolshevik military organizations such as Shaurov, who wrote: "The December Uprising in Moscow held important lessons for the entire SD organization, since it demonstrated the effects of inadequate preparation and lack of contact with the masses". I.V. Shaurov, "Pervaia konferentsiia voennykh i boevykh organizatsii RSDRP v Noiabre 1906 g", *Istoricheskii arkhiv* (1959); 160. Soviet historians continue to accept this interpretation. See L.G. Beskrovnyi, *Bor'ba bol'shevikov za armiiu v trekh revoliutsiiakh* (Moscow, 1969), pp.49–50.
27. Plekhanov was in the forefront of this movement which had attracted the support of Axelrod, Dan, and the majority of the Mensheviks. See Baron, *Plekhanov*, p.281.
28. *KPSS v rez.*, 1:176–7.
29. Ibid.
30. Ibid.
31. N. Ol'shauskii, "Podpol'naia rabota v armii v 1906 godu", *Rev i RKP (b)*, 4:334–41.
32. On the mid-century splendor of Kronstadt, see R. Delafield, *Report on the Art of War in Europe 1854, 1855, 1856* (Wash., D.C. House of Representatives, Dec. 1861), pp.24–33. Delafield rated Kronstadt "superior in execution and material and not inferior in design to any other in Europe". For conditions at the turn of the century see W.A. Macbean, *Handbook of the Military Forces of Russia* (London: HMSO, 1898), pp.112–14.
33. Pay rates are given in Macbean, p.55.
34. "Doklad Tov. Muskogo o sveaborgskom vosstanii", *Rev i RKP (b)*, 4:309–13.
35. "Vtoroe kronshtadskoe vosstanie", *Rev i RKP (b)*, 4:322–4, and N. Ol'shanskii, "Kronshtadtskoe vosstanie v 1906g.", *Krasnaia letopis'*, No. 5, 1923.
36. The program of the Union of officers of the Russian Army is included in "Podpol'-naia rabota v armii v 1906 godu", *Rev i RKP (b)*, 4:340. The group seems to have had little effect – its work certainly did not fulfill Menshevik expectations.
37. In Soviet histories the Bolshevik conference held at Tammerfors, 16–22 Nov. (29 Nov.–5 Dec.) 1906, has come to be called the *First* conference. In a sense this is correct, since this was a conference of Military *and Fighting* Organizations. The Menshevik conference had only included Military Organizations since fighting organizations had not been sanctioned by the Fourth Party Congress. The full protocols of the Menshevik conference apparently were never published, but a 13 page summary was printed by the Central Committee immediately after the conference. See *Lenin o voine*, 1:270 n. Lenin committed greater resources (probably reflecting one of the practical advantages of advocating expropriation) and published the full protocols of the November conference on his "Proletarii" press facility (St. Petersburg, 1907).
38. "Kratkoe izvlechenie iz protokolov 1-oi konferentsii organizatsii RSDRP

vedyshchikh rabotu v voiskakh" (St. Petersburg, 1906), and V.I. Lenin, "Po povodu protokolov noiabr'skoi voenno-boevoi konferentsii rossiskoi sotsial-demokraticheskoi rabochei partii" in *Rev i RKP (b)*, 4:341–7. This article originally appeared in *Proletarii*, No. 16 (2 May 1907).

39. "Predsmertnaia pesnia", *Soldatskaia Mysl'*, No. 2 (Oct. 1906), p.3.
40. "O vnutrennei voine", *Rev i RKP (b)*, 4:328–31.
41. Ibid., p.328.
42. Ibid., p.330.
43. Lenin had published an extensive article on partisan warfare in *Proletarii* in late September. See "Partizanskaia voina", *Lenin o voine*, 1:250–8.
44. The Tammerfors Conference was not purely Bolshevik. According to the memoir of one of the participants, the delegates included "one Menshevik who agreed with the Bolshevik program on the question of military organization". See I. V. Shaurov, "Pervaia konferentsiia voennykh i boevykh organizatsii RSDRP v Noiabre 1906g.", *Istoricheskii arkihiv*, 1(1950):160–71.
45. V.I. Lenin, "Po povodu protokolov noiabr'skoi voenno-boevoi konferentsii RSDRP", *Lenin o voine*, 1:270.
46. Only 28 delegates attended the conference, and of these nine could not vote. Eleven military and eight fighting organizations were represented: the military organizations of St. Petersburg, Kronstadt, Riga, Moscow, Finland, Sevastopol, Nizhni Novgorod, Kaluga, Voronezh, and Kazan, and the fighting organizations of St. Petersburg, Moscow, Saratov, and the Urals. See "Pervaia konferentsiia voennukh i boevykh organizatsii ESDRP", in *KPSS v rez.*, 1:192–202, which provides the evidence for the narrative which follows.
47. "Unit" was rather loosely defined. Essentially an army regiment or ship's crew was considered as a suitable level to strive for organizational effectiveness. These provided a large enough body of men so that a few potential SDs usually could be found, yet were small enough so that specific agitation and propaganda efforts could be developed to capitalize upon problems already known by the rank-and-file through barracks gossip.
48. See "Doklad Voronitsyna na konferentsii voennukh i boevykh organizatsii RSDRP", *Rev i RKP (b)*, 3:391–400, which develops this theme in an analysis of the Sevastopol uprising.
49. The real purpose of the conference comes into question here. Judging from the size of the conference and the apparent effect of propaganda efforts on the Imperial Army, there was little need for a new central organ. This leads to an interpretation which finds Lenin guilty of using the partisan warfare issue as a means of demonstrating his unwillingness to accede to Menshevik control. See Adam Ulam, *The Bolsheviks* (New York: Collier, 1965), pp.256–62. In this context the "need" springs from the continuing revolutionary enthusiasm of the people which the Central Committee has failed to recognize. The formation of pretentious organs such as the Temporary Bureau of Military and Fighting Organizations, having no basis in real need, is merely a device used to apply pressure on the delegates at the next Party Congress so that they will accept Lenin's tactics. Recent Soviet publications on the subject give evidence which challenges this interpretation by indicating that the military and fighting organizations were in fact quite large and needed a coordinating central agency. Shaurov's memoir, published in 1959, recalls that by June 1906 the Voronezh organization alone included more than 200 soldiers and counted on the support of more than 1500 sympathizers. In Voronezh the Party felt the workers in the city could rise without fear of the garrison because of the successful work of the military organization. The interpretational question cannot be resolved with the available evidence, but it appears that there was sufficient cause to form a central bureau to implement plans for the future even if past successes did not merit such action.
50. Deutscher, *The Prophet Armed*, p.177.
51. Ibid., p.179.
52. *KPSS v rez.*, 1:211.
53. Ibid., pp.218–19.

Notes

54. *Protokolyi Piatyi s"ezd RSDRP* (Moscow, 1933).
55. Deutscher, *The Prophet Armed*, p.178.
56. Trotsky wrote his "Itogi i Perspektivy" (now commonly called "Results and Prospects" but first translated into English under the title "A Review and some Perspectives") while awaiting trial after the arrest of the St. Petersburg Soviet. It was first published in 1906. The publishing history is given in L. Trotsky, *The Permanent Revolution and Results and Prospects* (New York: Pathfinder Press, 1969), p.25. Deutscher has called this work a peak in Trotsky's development which set the tone for all of his later intellectual effort. He summarized "Results and Prospects" in some detail in *The Prophet Armed* since he felt that it could have had an impact on European socialism equal to that of the *Communist Manifesto*. However, the treatment of the question of military power and the revolution set forth in "Results and Prospects" has not been analysed. See Deutscher, *The Prophet Armed*, pp.150–62.
57. Trotsky, *Permanent Revolution and Results and Prospects*, p.97.
58. Ibid.
59. Ibid.
60. Ibid., p.61.
61. Ibid.
62. Ibid., pp.110–11.
63. Ibid., p.112.

CHAPTER FOUR

1. Leon Trotsky, *My Life* (New York: Pathfinder, 1970), p.208.
2. Ibid., p.212.
3. Publication of Trotsky's *Pravda* began in October, 1908, and continued until May, 1912. By that time Lenin had appropriated the title for the Party newspaper being published in St. Petersburg, and the Viennese *Pravda* disappeared after an acrimonious exchange. See Isaac Deutscher, *The Prophet Armed* (New York: Random House, 1965), pp.198–9, Trotsky, *My Life*, p.220.
4. Trotsky had been a regular contributor to *Kievskaia Mysl'* since 1908, and the pay he had received for his columns had been an important part of his income during the Vienna period. See Trotsky, *My Life*, p.232. His columns had covered cultural as well as political topics. Written with an attractive combination of scholarship and wit, these journalistic pieces are still interesting today and must have resulted in a considerable readership at the time. See Trotsky, *Sochineniia*, 12 Vols. (Moscow, 1925–27), Vol. 20 (*Kultura Starogo Mira*), pp.267–400 for examples. Trotsky characterized *Kievsaia Mysl'* as a "popular radical paper of the Marxist hue" (*My Life*, p.230), but the most accurate of his chosen adjectives would appear to be "popular". It operated within the limits prescribed by tsarist censorship, and it appealed to readers who would have had little use for Trotsky's revolutionary programs.
5. Trotsky, *Sochineniia*, 6:6–13.
6. The political aspects of his reporting will be generally disregarded here. They are fully analysed in Deutscher, *The Prophet Armed*, pp.201–9.
7. This aspect of societal awareness of contemporary military conflict (war as "news") has not yet been systematically analysed. The origins of the war correspondent appear to be linked to the appearance of the cheap daily newspaper in the mid-nineteenth century, but the transition from the casual reporting of the periodical press to the competitive intensity of the daily press deserves study. Rupert Furneaux, *The Breakfast War* (New York: Thomas Crowell Company, 1958), provides an insight into the actions of military correspondents in their heyday by describing the reporting of the Russo-Turkish War of 1877–78. Lady Ellinor Grogan, *The Life of J.D. Bourchier* (London, 1926) gives a biographical description of the London *Times* correspondent who was the doyen of the war correspondents covering the Balkan Wars. See also Phillip Knightley, *The First*

Casualty. From the Crimea to Vietnam: The War Correspondent as Hero, Propagandist, and Myth Maker (New York, 1975).

8. Trotsky, *Sochineniia*, 6:244.
9. The exact date of Trotsky's arrival in the Balkans cannot be determined. In his autobiography he merely states that "in September 1912, I was on my way to the East, believing that war was not only probable but inevitable" (*My Life*, p.226). Deutscher says that "early in October he left Vienna; and in a cab on the way to the station he learned of the outbreak of the first Balkan War, in which the southern Slavs joined hands against the Turkish empire" (*The Prophet Armed*, p.201). The contradiction between the two accounts is not as great as it would appear. Trotsky obviously was refreshing his memory with the articles he had published at the time of the war, which carried Old Style dates. Deutscher apparently is considering the Montenegran declaration of war on Turkey (8 October, 1912) as the beginning of the First Balkan War even though war did not actually break out until 18 October. Internal evidence in Trotsky's columns indicates that he arrived in Belgrade on 10 or 11 October (27 or 28 September Old Style) (*Sochineniia*, 6:62–68, 82). He stayed there until the morning of October 18, when he left for Sofia. This was the day Trotsky (and most historians) considered as the beginning of the war, and he wrote extensively about his experiences on that memorable day (*Sochineniia*, 6:134–44). He stayed in Sofia until hostilities ended and then returned to Vienna until the Second Balkan War erupted. He returned to Sofia to report the war and then spent several weeks in Rumania before returning to Vienna. See Trotsky, *My Life*, pp.227–8; Deutscher, *The Prophet Armed*, p.205.
10. Trotsky, *Sochineniia*, 6:63.
11. Ibid., p.62.
12. Ibid., pp.64–8.
13. Ibid., p.173.
14. Ibid., pp.211–17. Trotsky discussed this problem in greatest detail in his writings on Russian diplomatic attitudes toward Bulgaria.
15. Ibid., p.71.
16. Ibid., pp.128–9.
17. Ibid., p.129. This appeared in *Kievskaia Mysl'* on 24 Oct. (6 Nov.) 1912, well before hostilities developed between Bulgaria and her allies.
18. Ibid., pp.66–7.
19. Ibid., p.120.
20. Ibid., p.187.
21. Ibid.
22. Ibid., p.185.
23. Definitions of "strategy" are numerous. Those used here are derived from the Introduction to Edward Mead Earle, ed., *Makers of Modern Strategy* (New York: Atheneum, 1967), p.viii.
24. Trotsky, *Sochineniia*, 6:151.
25. Ibid., pp.145–7.
26. Ibid., p.151.
27. Ibid., p.172.
28. Ibid., p.152.
29. Trotsky did not investigate Turkish strategic alternatives before the battle of Kirkilisse, even though this would have added more weight to his argument that time was the critical factor. After the Young Turk revolt of 1908 the Turkish General Staff had worked out a contingency plan to be implemented if a Balkan Alliance threatened Turkish sovereignty. This plan called for Turkish forces to assume the defensive in the critical theater between Adrianople and Constantinople until reinforcements could be brought from Asia Minor. However, when war broke out in 1912 the Turks became bold when the Bulgarians failed to attack immediately. They initiated an offensive which ended disastrously, so weakening the defenses at Kirkilisse that these were taken by the Bulgarians after only one day's fighting (22–23 October 1912). See Ernst C. Helmreich, *The Diplomacy of the Balkan Wars, 1912–1913* (Cambridge, 1938), pp.193–5; Philip Howell, *The Cam-*

paign in Thrace, 1912 (London, 1913), pp.63–70; Historical Section, The German Great General Staff, *The Balkan War, 1912–1913*, trans. by Harry Bell (Leavenworth, 1914), pp.33–56.
30. Trotsky, *Sochineniia*, 6:150–2.
31. Adrianople held one sixth of Turkey's peacetime military establishment in the Balkans. Its defenses were composed of 17 mutually supporting fortresses encompassing a perimeter of 40 kilometers (ibid.). Many of these troops were assigned to fortress artillery units and would not have been capable of participating in offensive operations, but the remainder was still a large force which could not be ignored with impunity.
32. Ibid., p.150.
33. Ibid., p.151.
34. Ibid., p.151. Trotsky's assessment apparently was not perfectly accurate. The Turks retreated from Kirkilisse in disorder, but the Bulgarian failure to pursue allowed the Turkish generals to restore order. The result matched Trotsky's perceptions. See German General Staff, *The Balkan War*, pp.52–3.
35. Ibid., pp.151–2.
36. Ibid., p.152.
37. Ibid.
38. Ibid. The wall of Anastasius had been built during the reign of Anastasius I (491–518) to protect Constantinople against the inroads of the Slavic Getae. See *The Cambridge Medieval History*, Vol. I, *The Christian Roman Empire* (New York, Macmillan Company, 1911), Map 6. The Turks had in fact prepared their defensive lines a few miles further to the rear, near the town of Chataldja, where the terrain was slightly more favorable and the defensive line could be shorter.
39. Ibid., pp.152–3.
40. The campaign is outlined in Lt. Col. E. Boucabeille, *La guerre interbalkanique: événements militaires et politiques survenus dans la Péninsule des Balkans jusqu'en octobre 1913* (Paris, 1913), pp.57–71. Howell, *The Campaign in Thrace* and German General Staff, *The Balkan War* give, respectively, Bulgarian and Turkish views.
41. The Bulgarians detached an army corps from their forces in Thrace in an attempt to reach Salonika before the Greeks. See D.J. Cassavetti, *Hellas and the Balkan Wars* (New York, 1914), p.87.
42. Trotsky, *Sochineniia*, 6:115.
43. Cf. Trotsky, *My Life*, pp.114–23; Deutscher, *The Prophet Armed*, p.148.
44. Trotsky, *Sochineniia*, 6:200.
45. Ibid., pp.224–5.
46. Ibid., pp.218–23.
47. Ibid., p.225.
48. Ibid., p.64.
49. Ibid., p.65.
50. Leon Trotsky, "There and Back" in *1905*, pp.429–75.
51. Trotsky, *Sochineniia*, 6:120.
52. Ibid.
53. Ibid., p.122.
54. Ibid., p.124.
55. Ibid., p.123.
56. Ibid., p.116.
57. Ibid., p.180. Neither the Bulgarian nor the Serbian army had strong cavalry arms, and Trotsky did not attempt to assess the value of mounted troops in his analysis of the Balkan Wars. See Lancelot Lawton, "A German View of the Turkish Defeat", *Fortnightly Review* (May 1913) XCIII New Series, pp.975–87 for an account of cavalry inadequacies. Howell, *The Campaign in Thrace*, 37–41, 58–9, 126–31 provides an ardent, though rather unconvincing argument for cavalry in modern warfare.
58. Ibid., p.116.
59. Ibid., pp.180–1. When interviewing wounded Bulgarian soldiers in Sofia, Trotsky

was only seeing those who had been lightly wounded. The Bulgarians used a system of medical treatment designed to limit the distance travelled by men who had severe wounds, and most of these were moved no further to the rear than Philippopolis. Turkish artillery shells had a tendency to wound a man only lightly if he was not hit directly. This may help to explain the preponderance of men who had suffered artillery wounds being treated in the hospitals of Sofia.

60. Ibid., p.181.
61. Ibid., p.125. The Turks were using a projectile with a heavy bursting charge which exploded with such great force that the shell fragments were too tiny to have serious effect.
62. Ibid., p.181.
63. Ibid., p.202.

CHAPTER FIVE

1. The Vienna interlude is described in Leon Trotsky, *My Life* (New York: Pathfinder Press, 1970), pp.238–42. Trotsky's role in Switzerland is found in Alfred E. Senn, *The Russian Revolution in Switzerland* (Madison: University of Wisconsin Press, 1971), pp.152–5.
2. Leon Trotsky, "War and the International", in Isaac Deutscher, ed., *The Age of Permanent Revolution: A Trotsky Anthology* (New York: Dell Publishing Company, 1964), p.79.
3. Trotsky, *My Life*, p.237.
4. Ibid., p.243.
5. Ibid.
6. Isaac Deutscher, *The Prophet Armed* (New York: Random House, 1965), pp.220–1, gives an account of the political orientation of the newspaper's editorial staff.
7. R.V. Daniels, *Red October: The Bolshevik Revolution of 1917* (New York: Charles Scribner's Sons, 1967), pp.26–7.
8. Leon Trotsky, *My Life*, pp.252–7.
9. Most of these newspaper columns were reproduced in Vol. 9, "Evropa v voine", of Trotsky's *Sochineniia* or in *Gody velikago pereloma* (Moscow: 1919). A few of the less important columns appearing in *Kievskaia Mysl'* were not reproduced in either work. Most of these are available in the Slavic Collection of the New York Public Library, but those holdings are not complete.
10. An excellent example of Trotsky's descriptive genius is "'Sedmoi pekhotnyi' v Bel'giiskoi epopee", *Sochineniia*, 9:58–74, which tells the story of the fall of Belgium as it was seen by a member of the Belgian army. Deutscher does not exaggerate when he introduces his discussion of this essay by writing that "If the fate of Trotsky's writings ... and the extent to which they are read or ignored had not been so inseparably bound up with his political fortunes and with the sympathies and the antipathies that his mere name evokes, he would have had his niche in literature on the strength of these writings alone". See Deutscher, *The Prophet Armed*, pp.230–1.
11. Trotsky, *Sochineniia*, 9:142–3.
12. Ibid., p.143. Emphasis in the original.
13. Ibid., p.37.
14. Ibid., p.10.
15. Ibid., p.9.
16. Ibid., p.10.
17. Ibid., p.36.
18. Ibid., p.11.
19. Ibid., pp.9–11.
20. Ibid., p.9.
21. Ibid., p.11.
22. Ibid., p.12.
23. Ibid.

Notes

24. Ibid., p.37.
25. Ibid., p.218.
26. Ibid., p.246.
27. Leon Trotsky, *Gody velikago pereloma*, 3 vols. in 1 (Moscow, 1919), Vol. 3: "Voina i tekhnika", p.101.
28. Ibid., p.102.
29. Ibid., pp.102–3.
30. While the article was published as an interview, the respondent was "Captain Jean de Vin-Rouge", recovering in an infirmary after having been severely wounded at the front. Since the name arouses more than a little suspicion, one can only conclude that Trotsky was drawing upon observations made during hospital visits and had developed a composite respondent so that he could gain the dramatic impact of using the first person in his descriptive passages.
31. Ibid., pp.104–5.
32. Ibid., p.106.
33. Ibid., p.107.
34. Ibid., p.108.
35. Ibid.
36. Ibid.
37. Ibid., p.109.
38. Trotsky, *The Age of Permanent Revolution* ed. Isaac Deutscher, p.83.
39. Trotsky, *Sochineniia*, 9:220.
40. Ibid., p.133.
41. Ibid., p.148. This was published in *Nashe Slovo* one week before the Zimmerwald Conference and reflects the stand Trotsky was to take there. He rejected Lenin's slogan, "Turn the imperialist war into civil war", arguing that the war should end "without victor or vanquished". See Deutscher, *The Prophet Armed*, p.226.
42. Ibid., p.36.
43. Ibid. In this comment Trotsky rejects the classic interpretation of military historians which gives the German General Staff credit for relatively innovative thought in using its reserve formations alongside regulars in the opening phases of the war. See B.H. Liddell Hart, *The Real War, 1914–1918* (Boston: Little, Brown and Company, 1964), pp.36–40.
44. Ibid., p.17.
45. Ibid., p.220.
46. Ibid., p.36. Trotsky was still "Antid Oto" to the readers of *Kievskaia Mysl'*, and his tendency to try to serve as an antidote to the optimistic hopes for rapid victory being voiced in the official press should not be overlooked.
47. Trotsky, *Age of Permanent Revolution*, p.80.
48. Trotsky, *Sochineniia*, 9:187.
49. Ibid., p.191. Trotsky dated this innovation from the French offensive in Champagne in September of 1915. Since the innovation was not as dramatic as Trotsky made it sound, it is rather difficult to date precisely. However, artillery fire was in fact used in the manner Trotsky described in that offensive. See *Les Armées Françaises dans la Grande Guerre*, Vol. 3 (Paris: Imprimerie Nationale, 1923), pp.356–64.
50. Trotsky, *Sochineniia*, 9:192.
51. Ibid., p.190.
52. Ibid.
53. Ibid., p.189.
54. Ibid., p.190.
55. Ibid.
56. Ibid.
57. Ibid.
58. Leon Trotsky, *Gody velikago pereloma*, p.57.
59. Trotsky, *Sochineniia*, 9:191–2.
60. Ibid., p.40.
61. Ibid.

62. Ibid., p.192.
63. Ibid., p.193.
64. Ibid.
65. Ibid.
66. Trotsky's awareness of the significance of technology led him to study artillery quite carefully since this was a field in which developments not only had military implications but also impacted on the mobilized civilian economy. The degree of his understanding of the weapons system is reflected in his description of the use of artillery to fire against targets acquired by aviators' observations of the enemy-held area. Machines clearly were changing the nature of warfare when this technique was used, for it allowed the modern warrior to see and strike further than had ever been possible before. L. Trotsky, "Pis'ma s zapada: Zapiski soldata", *Kievskaia Mysl'* 14 Feb. 1915.
67. Trotsky, *Sochineniia*, 9:193–4.
68. Ibid., p.194.
69. Ibid., p.195.
70. Ibid.
71. Ibid.
72. Ibid.
73. Ibid.

CHAPTER SIX

1. Leon Trotsky, *My Life* (New York: Pathfinder Press, 1970), pp.270–8.
2. Leon Trotsky, *Sochineniia*, 12 Vols. (Moscow, 1925–27), Vol. 3 (*1917*), Part 1 (*Ot Fevralia do Oktiabria*), p.6.
3. Ibid., pp.6–7.
4. Ibid., p.13.
5. Ibid., p.18.
6. Ibid., p.33. Also Trotsky, *My Life*, pp.279–85.
7. Trotsky, *My Life*, p.287.
8. Trotsky's first speech to the Petrograd Soviet is in *Sochineniia*, Vol. 3, Part 1:45–6. The relationship between Lenin and Trotsky on matters of political methods rather than interpretation of events has been investigated in great detail by others and purposely has been omitted here. See Isaac Deutscher, *The Prophet Armed* (New York: Random House, 1965), pp.249–59; Adam Ulam, *The Bolsheviks* (New York: Collier Books, 1968), pp.337–8; Robert Daniels, *The Conscience of the Revolution* (Cambridge: Harvard University Press, 1960), pp.46–8. Trotsky's speeches and articles of May 1917 indicate acceptance of the need to manipulate men and events for the success of the revolution. Few theoretical differences separated Trotsky and Lenin. Both were willing to act to facilitate the revolution, and they seldom differed on methods. Trotsky's combination of oratorical and journalistic skills made his approach seem more open than Lenin's, especially when viewed in retrospect. But both men were using their own approach to accelerate the world revolution which they felt was close at hand.
9. Trotsky, *My Life*, p.288.
10. George Katkov, *Russia, 1917: The February Revolution* (New York: Harper and Row, 1967), p.270. Also S. Rabinovich, "Bol'shevistskie voennye organizatsii v 1917g", *Proletarskaia Revoliutsiia*, 1928, Nos. 6–7, p.180, and A.A. Pitul'ko, "Bor'ba bolshevikov za soldatskie massy petrogradskogo garnizona v period mirnogo razvitiia revoliutsii", ed. E.I. Mikhlin, *Lenin – Partiia – Oktiabr'* (Leningrad, 1967), pp.146–65.
11. On plans see William Henry Chamberlin, *The Russian Revolution, 1917–1921*, 2 vols. (New York: Macmillan Co., 1963), 1:74 and Alexander Rabinowitch, *Prelude to Revolution: The Petrograd Bolsheviks and the July 1917 Uprising* (Bloomington: Indiana University Press, 1968), p.24. On memoirs see Katkov, p.282.
12. The description of conditions and attitudes in fortresses and the Baltic Fleet which

Notes

follows has been constructed from "Armiia v period podgotovki i provedeniia velikoi oktiabr'skoi sotsialisticheskoi revoliutsii", *Krasnyi Arkhiv*, 5 (New Series) (1937): 136–87; "Revoliutsionnaia propaganda v armii v 1916–1917 gg.", *Krasnyi Arkhiv*, 17 (1926): 36–50; "Russkaia armiia nakanune revoliutsii", *Byloe*, 1918, No. 7, pp.151–7; F.F. Raskol'nikov, *Kronshtadt i Piter v 1917 godu* (Moscow, 1925), pp.12–55; and Kh. I. Muratov, *Revoliutsionnoe dvizhenie v russkoi armii v 1917 godu* (Moscow, 1958), pp.5–18.

13. Chamberlin, p.85.
14. Ibid., p.113.
15. Oskar Anweiler, *The Soviets: The Russian Workers, Peasants and Soldiers Councils, 1905–1921*, trans. by Ruth Hein (New York: Pantheon Books, 1974), pp.139–43.
16. Trotsky, *Sochineniia*, 3, Part 1:51.
17. Ibid., p.55.
18. Ibid., pp.107–8.
19. One of the continuing problems in the relationship between the garrison and the Provisional Government was the question of troop levies from Petrograd. The decree establishing the authority of the Provisional Government had included the provision, "The military units which took part in the revolutionary movement are not to be disarmed or removed from Petrograd". (The document is reproduced in its entirety in Chamberlin, pp.431–2.) This position was sound at the time for it overcame fears of retribution and facilitated a return to normal conditions in the capital. As time passed it became less useful, for demands from the front required replacements to pass through the Petrograd training base. While members of the Provisional Government recognized that revocation of the decree would lead to violent mutinies in the garrison, they argued that "units" should not be construed to mean individual replacements, and thus levies should continue. Radical critics of the government told the garrison that the right to extract levies would in fact be the right to remove individuals who supported the revolution. The attempt to levy the 1st Machine Gun Regiment was one of the proximate causes of the July demonstrations. See Rabinowitch, pp.135–40.
20. Trotsky, *Sochineniia*, 3, Part 1: 108.
21. Ibid., pp.124–32.
22. Ibid., p.126.
23. Ibid.
24. Ibid., p.127.
25. Ibid.
26. Ibid.
27. Ibid., pp.141–4.
28. Leon Trotsky, *The History of the Russian Revolution*, 3 vols., trans. by Max Eastman (New York: Simon & Schuster, 1932), 1:138.
29. Pitul'ko, pp.147–8.
30. See V.I. Nevsky, "Voennaia organizatsiia i oktiabr'skaia revoliutsiia", *Krasnoarmeets*, Nos. 10–15, 1919, p.34.
31. Pitul'ko, pp.155–7.
32. Ibid.
33. All members of the Bolshevik Military Organization were required to join the Party and subordinate themselves to Party discipline. This gave the Party some insurance against divergence between its "military line" and "civilian line", but this was not a simple matter. Working with rank and file soldiers put the Bolshevik Military Organization members in contact with an audience highly receptive to the most radical slogans. As a result these members tended to be to the left of the Party members with civilian "constituencies". They never achieved autonomy, though, and in retrospect were willing to admit that this gave them an advantage over other parties, especially the SRs, who allowed their "front" and "rear" propaganda lines to diverge and lost credibility in the process. See Rabinovich, pp.187–92: "Vserossiiskaia konferentsiia frontovykh i tylovykh voennykh organizatsii RSDRP (b)", Petrograd 16–23 June (29 June–6 July) 1917 in *Kommunisticheskaia partiia*

sovetskogo soiuza v rezoliutsiiakh i resheniiakh s″ezdov, konferentsii i plenumov Tsk, Vol. I (1898–1917) (Moscow, 1970), pp.465–79.

34. Trotsky, *History of the Russian Revolution*, 1:184.
35. The parliamentary relationship between the Soviet and the army was complex. Trotsky's description was straightforward: "At the session of March 6, the Executive Committee considered it advisable to install its own commissars in all regiments and all military institutions. Thus was created a threefold bond between the soldier and the Soviet: the regiments sent their representatives to the Soviet; the Executive Committee sent its commissars to the regiments; and finally at the head of each regiment stood an elective committee, constituting a sort of lower nucleus of the Soviet". *History of the Russian Revolution*, 1:294. This is accurate as far as it goes, but soldiers' committees were set up at all echelons above the regiment. The same system of direct election employed at lower levels was used to form the divisional committees, but committees at corps, army, and front were formed using indirect methods based upon the percentage of each party's representation on committees at the next lower echelon. See Rabinovich, p.186.
36. Trotsky, *Sochineniia*, 3, Part 1:132–5. The June 10th Demonstration had been planned by the Bolsheviks to take advantage of worker unrest in Petrograd following conflict between the Provisional Government and a group of Anarchist-Communists on 7–8 June. Serious violence had been avoided when the Petrograd Soviet successfully mediated the conflict, but tempers were running high and Bolshevik leaders organized an anti-government street demonstration. This course of action was denounced by the Executive Committee of the Petrograd Soviet and the All-Russian Congress of Soviets. The Bolsheviks bowed to the wishes of these organizations and cancelled the demonstration. See Rabinowitch, pp.64–80.
37. Chamberlin, 1:142.
38. Katkov, pp.366–7.
39. V.I. Startsev, *Ocherki po istorii petrogradskoi krasnoi gvardii i rabochei militsii (Mart 1917–Aprel' 1918)* (Moscow, 1965), p.85.
40. G.A. Tsypkin, *Krasnaia gvardiia v bor'be za vlast' sovetov* (Moscow, 1967), p.27.
41. S.N. Valk, R. Sh. Ganelin, *et al.*, eds., *Oktiabr'skoe vooruzhennoe vosstanie: semnadtsatyi god v petrograde*, 2 vols. (Leningrad, 1967), 1:124–5.
42. Ibid., pp.126–8.
43. Ibid., p.124. See also A.G. Shliapnikov, *Semnadtsatyi god*, 4 vols. (Moscow, 1923), 1:235–42.
44. See N. Rostov, "Voznikhovenie krasnoi gvardii", *Krasnaia Nov'*, Feb. 1927, pp.168–80.
45. Ibid. See also Shliapnikov, 1:240–53.
46. Rostov, p.170.
47. The term "Red Guard" had been used in 1905 and had reappeared in an 18 March *Pravda* article by Bonch Bruevich. See Startsev, p.103. Rostov's "Project to Organize the Red Guards" provides some useful insights into contemporary hopes for a properly-constituted militia.

> 1. The Red Guards have been formed for the defense of the gains of the revolution and for the struggle against counter-revolutionary activity. In their actions the Red Guards proceed in complete unity with the Soviet of Workers and Soldiers Deputies.
> 2. The membership of the Red Guard will be made up of workers recommended by the socialist parties.
> 3. The Red Guard will be formed from regional (*raionnye*) druzhinas.
> 4. The regional druzhinas will be formed from sub-regional detachments.
> 5. Sub-regional detachments from hundreds (companies).
> 6. Hundreds from tens.
> 7. At the head of the ten (*desiatok*) there will be a squad leader.
> 8. A council of squad leaders will elect the company commander.
> 9. The company commanders will elect the detachment commander.
> 10. Detachment commanders will elect the druzhina commander.

Notes

11. Druzhina commanders will elect the Red Guard commander.
12. Every member of the Red Guard will be responsible to a squad leader.
13. It is the duty of the squad leader councils to invite experienced instructors to work with the druzhinas.
14. All applications for membership in the Red Guard will be considered in a council of squad leaders. Unfavorable decisions by this council may be appealed to a general meeting.
15. Squad leaders are responsible for the precise execution of instruction.
16. Those guilty of disobeying instructions will be stricken from the rolls of the Red Guard by the council of squad leaders, sanctioned by a general meeting (Rostov, p.171).

48. Trotsky, *Sochineniia*, 3, Part 1:134.

CHAPTER SEVEN

1. Leon Trotsky, *Lessons of October* (New York: Pioneer Publishers, 1937), p.55. The role of the Bolshevik Party in planning and directing the July Demonstrations is covered in more detail and with more objectivity in Alexander Rabinowitch, *Prelude to Revolution: The Petrograd Bolsheviks and the July 1917 Uprising* (Bloomington: Indiana University Press, 1968), pp.135–76.
2. Leon Trotsky, *Sochineniia*, 12 Vols. (Moscow, 1925–27), Vol. 3 (*1917*), Part 1 (*Ot Fevralia do Oktiabria*), p.198.
3. Ibid., p.195.
4. Ibid., p.139. See also Rabinowitch, p.139.
5. Trotsky, *Sochineniia*, 3, Part 1:197.
6. Trotsky, *My Life* (New York: Pathfinder Press, 1970), p.311.
7. See Rabinowitch, pp.169–70, for this interpretation.
8. The concept of "Soviet legality" is most fully developed in Trotsky, *Lessons of October*, pp.83–7. In essence, the concept implies a parliamentary function for the Soviet in the peculiar conditions of *dvoevlastie*. Legitimacy in government had passed to the Provisional Government, but in actual practice all parties recognized the right of the Soviet to alter decrees issued by the Provisional Government. This implied a "constitutional" role for the Soviet and gave it an ability to provide legal sanction. Decisions of the Soviet could be considered as having the force of law in dealings between the Soviet and political parties or interest groups. In the specific case of the July Days the concept of "Soviet legality" would require the cancellation of the demonstration if it was unacceptable to the Soviet. The difficulty encountered in attempting to apply this concept in analysing Trotsky's actions on 3 July springs from the fact that he did not clearly articulate it until much later and then only used it to justify his actions when he controlled the majority of the Soviet.
9. This is one of the best-told tales of Trotsky's revolutionary exploits. See Isaac Deutscher, *The Prophet Armed* (New York: Random House, 1965), pp.271–3, and L. Trotsky, *My Life*, pp.312–13.
10. Rabinowitch, p.199. Trotsky, *History of the Russian Revolution*, 3 vols., trans. by Max Eastman (New York: Simon & Schuster, 1932), 2:49. Trotsky confused the units involved in the rescue of the Soviet when recounting the July Days in *My Life*. There he names the Volhynian Regiment as the defenders of the status quo. This error may have been a deliberate dramatic device, for he gives the same regiment credit for a leading role in the October Revolution, thus neatly demonstrating the reversal in attitudes among military men between July and October. See Trotsky, *My Life*, p.313.
11. Adam Ulam, *The Bolsheviks* (New York: Collier Books, 1965), pp.349–50, provides a good summary of the charges and Lenin's responses.
12. Marcel Liebman, *The Russian Revolution*, trans. by Arnold J. Pomerans (New York: Random House, 1970), p.188.
13. Trotsky, *Sochineniia*, 3, Part 1: 163–5.

14. Ibid., pp.165–6.
15. Ibid., p.168.
16. Ibid., p.167.
17. Ibid., p.169.
18. Deutscher, pp.278–9.
19. The historical record is not totally convincing on this point. Rabinowitch, in his *Prelude to Revolution*, relies on Shumiatsky's memoir in asserting that Trotsky was among those who argued for the dissolution of the Military Organization at the Sixth Party Congress which met in Petrograd, 26 July–3 August. Cf. B. Shumiatsky, "Shestoi s"ezd partii i rabochii klass", in *V dni proletarskoi revoliutsii* (Moscow, 1937), p.93. However, the date of publication of this memoir makes it a suspect source for Trotsky's actions, and as Rabinowitch notes (p.203), "The positions of Trotsky and Kamenev must have been made known through intermediaries since both were still in prison at the time of the Congress". Records of the Congress are fragmentary because continuing anti-Bolshevik actions required a modicum of secrecy. See *Shestoi s"ezd RSDRP (bol'shevikov), avgust 1917 goda: Protokoly* (Moscow, 1958), pp.270–90.
20. Deutscher, p.282.
21. F.F. Raskol'nikov, "V tiur'me kerensogo", *Proletarskaia Revoliutsiia* 10 (22), 1923, pp.155–7.
22. Liebman, p.195.
23. Ibid., p.202. See also Donald Treadgold, *Twentieth Century Russia*, 2nd Edition (Chicago: Rand McNally & Company, 1964), p.134.
24. Trotsky, *Russian Revolution*, 2:151.
25. V.I. Startsev, *Ocherki po istorii petrogradskoi krasnoi gvardii i rabochei militsii (Mart 1917–Aprel' 1918g.)* (Moscow, 1965), pp.164–5.
26. Ibid., p.98.
27. While the factory militia had a defensive role, perceptive military planners of the Left saw the factory sites as "strategic" points since they usually were located on railways, canals, or major thoroughfares and often commanded all types of communication which would be important if fighting erupted. See A. Antonov, "Imenem voenno-revoliutsionnogo komiteta", *Novyi Mir*, 10 (1957): 165.
28. Startsev, p.98.
29. V.D. Bonch-Bruevich, *Na boevykh postakh fevral'skoi i oktiabr'skoi revoliutsii* (Moscow, 1931), p.140.
30. Startsev, p.167.
31. Trotsky, *Sochineniia*, 3, Part 1: 153–6.
32. Deutscher, p.281.
33. Norman Stone, *The Eastern Front, 1914–1917* (New York: Charles Scribner's Sons, 1975) p.282.
34. Trotsky, *Sochineniia*, 3, Part 2: 256–69.
35. F.A. Golder, ed., *Documents of Russian History, 1914–1917* (New York: Century Company, 1927), pp.580–2.
36. Startsev, pp.167–8. The Red Guards in the Viborg District had 70 instructors for a 4000-man organization in September. Thirty of the instructors were from the Bolshevik Military Organization; the remainder were local workers who were in the army.
37. Startsev, p.171.
38. L.S. Gaponenko, ed., *Velikii Oktiabr': Sbornik dokumentov* (Moscow, 1961), p.243. See also Robert V. Daniels, *Red October: The Bolshevik Revolution of 1917* (New York: Charles Scribner's Sons, 1967), p.81. Daniels asserts that "the Red Guards did not even have a city-wide organization yet" on 15 October.
39. The All-Russian Democratic Conference was convened by the Mensheviks and other moderate socialist groups in an effort to regain the ground they were losing in the Soviet as attitudes drifted toward the left. Delegations from political and non-political organizations met in Petrograd beginning on 14 September. The political implications for Trotsky and the Bolsheviks are found in Deutscher, pp.283–6.
40. Trotsky, *Sochineniia*, 3, Part 1: 293.

Notes

41. Ibid., p.297.
42. Ibid., pp.314–16.
43. Ibid., pp.349–51.
44. Ibid., pp.320–1.
45. Daniels, p.72.
46. Trotsky, *Sochineniia*, 3, Part 2: 8–10.
47. S. Piontkovskii, "Voenno-revoliutsionnyi komitet v oktiabr'skie dni", *Proletarskaia revoliutsiia*, 10 (69), 1927, pp.111–12.
48. D.A. Chugaev, et al., eds., *Petrogradskii voenno-revoliutsionnyi komitet: dokumety i materialy*, 3 vols. (Moscow, 1966), 1:38–9.
49. Daniels, pp.49–80. Trotsky was engaged in both debates, and the ambiguity of his position is a major source of the continuing controversy over his political role in the October Revolution. Trotsky's detractors argue that his attempt to link the uprising to the Congress of Soviets is evidence of his obstructionism and lack of revolutionary insight. Cf. A.M. Andreev, *Sovety rabochikh i soldatskikh deputatov nakanune oktiabria (Mart–Oktiabr' 1917g)* (Moscow, 1967), pp.372–3. Trotsky argued that this linkage was just as essential as the notion that the insurrectionary preparations were actually a Soviet defensive function rather than a Party effort. See Trotsky, *Lessons of October*, p.83.
50. Chugaev, 1:41.
51. Trotsky, *Sochineniia*, 3, Part 2: 15.
52. Piontkovskii, pp.113–15.
53. Startsev, pp.184, 188–9.
54. Chugaev, 1:56–61. Commissars were sent to regiments and separate battalions to provide liaison while determining military capabilities and levels of personnel and supply availability.
55. Trotsky, *Sochineniia*, 3, Part 2: 34–5.
56. Chugaev, 1:63.
57. Trotsky, *Sochineniia*, 3, Part 2: 41–2.
58. Chugaev, 1:64.
59. Ibid., p.97.
60. Ibid., pp.81–2.
61. Trotsky, *Sochineniia*, 3, Part 2: 59.
62. Ibid., p.69.
63. Ibid., pp.87–8.
64. Ibid., pp.306–8.
65. Ibid., pp.309–10.

Selected Bibliography

I. ARCHIVES CONSULTED

The Trotsky Archives (Houghton Library, Harvard University). The earliest document in this collection is dated 31 January 1918, so it provided no material of direct applicability to the period studied here. However, a number of the manuscripts and unpublished documents in Sections A and B (covering the period before 1930) gave insight into Trotsky's retrospective thoughts on events before October 1917.

The Labadie Collection (University of Michigan). Only a small part of this collection, that which deals with Leftist fighting organizations before 1917, was of real value.

The Slavic Collection (New York Public Library). The collection of Bolshevik newspapers, periodicals, and memoirs made this an important source of materials. It was especially useful for the chapters on 1917.

II. BIBLIOGRAPHIES

In addition to the standard finding aids used by students of Russian history the following were especially useful in this study.

Akhun, M.I. and Petrov, V. *1917 god vo petrograde: khronika sobytii i bibliografiia.* Leningrad, 1933.

Dobranitskyi, M. *Sistematicheskii ukazatal literatury po istorii russkoi revoliutsii.* Moscow, 1926.

Lebedev, V.A. *Normalnyi katalog krasnoarmeiskoi biblioteki.* Moscow, 1928.

Oborona SSSR i krasnaia armiia: katalog knig. Moscow–Leningrad, 1928.

Postnikov, S.P. *Bibliografiia Russkoi revoliutsii, grazhdanskoi voiny, 1917–1921.* Prague, 1938.

Sinclair, Louis, *Leon Trotsky: A Bibliography.* Stanford, 1972.

III. TROTSKY'S WRITINGS

The Age of Permanent Revolution: A Trotsky Anthology. Edited by Isaac Deutscher. New York, 1964.

Gody velikogo pereloma. 3 Vs. in 1. Moscow–Petrograd–Nizhni Novgorod, 1919.

The History of the Russian Revolution. 3 Vols. Trans. Max Eastman. New York, 1932.

Lenin. Trans. Max Eastman. New York, 1925.

Leon Trotsky Speaks. Ed. Sarah Lovell. New York, 1972.

Lessons of October. Trans. John G. Wright. New York, 1937.

My Life: An Attempt at an Autobiography. New York, 1970.

1905. Trans. Anya Bostock. New York, 1972.

Our Revolution: Essays on Working-class and International Revolution, 1904–1917. New York, 1918.

The Permanent Revolution and Results and Prospects. Trans. Brian Pearce. New

Selected Bibliography

York, 1969.
Perspektivyi russkoi revoliutsii. Berlin, 1917.
Sochineniia. 12 Vols. Moscow–Leningrad, 1925–1927.
The Trotsky Papers, 1917–1921. Ed. and annotated by Jan M. Meijer, The Hague, 1964–1972.
Voina i revoliutsiia: krushenie vtorogo internatsionala i podgotovka tret'ega. 2 Vols. Petrograd, 1922–1924.

IV. PUBLISHED DOCUMENTS AND DOCUMENTARY COLLECTIONS

"Arkhivnyie materialnyi po armii v 1917 gody". *Krasnyi Arkhiv* (1927) 23:3–70. 24:71–107.
"Armiia v period podgotovki i provedeniia velikoi oktiabr'skoi sotsialisticheskoi revoliutsii". *Krasnyi Arkhiv* (1927) 5 (84):136–87.
The Bolsheviks and the October Revolution: Minutes of the Central Committee of the Russian Social-Democratic Labor Party (bolsheviks) August 1917–February 1918. Trans. Ann Bone. London, 1974.
Bunyan, James and Fisher, H.H. Compilers. *The Bolshevik Revolution, 1917–1918: Documents and Materials.* Stanford, 1934.
Chaadaeva, O.N., ed. *Soldatskie pis'ma 1917 goda.* Moscow, 1927.
Chernenko, K.U. and Svinkin, N.I., eds. *KPSS o vooruzhennykh silakh sovetskogo soiuza (Dokumenty, 1917–1968).* Moscow, 1969.
Chugaev, D.A. et al., eds. *Petrogradskii veonno-revoliutsionnyi komitet.* 3 Vols. Moscow, 1966.
Drezen, A.K., ed. *Bol'shevizatsiia petrogradskogo garnizona: sbornik materialov i dokumentov.* Moscow–Leningrad, 1932.
——. "Petrogradskii garnizon v oktiabre (materialy)". *Krasnaia Letopis* (1927) 2 (23):101–3.
Elagin, V.L. "K istorii oktiabr'skikh dnei v petrograde (iz materialov petrogradskogo voenno-revoliutsionnogo komiteta)". *Krasnyi Arkhiv* (1932) 4 (53): 38–62.
Gankin, Olga H. and Fisher, H.H., eds. *The Bolsheviks and the World War: The Origins of the Third International.* Stanford, 1940.
Gaponenko, L.S., ed. *Revoliutsionnoe dvizhenie v Russkoi armii, 27 fevraliia–24 oktiabria 1917 goda: sbornik dokumentov.* Moscow, 1968.
——, ed. *Velikii oktiabr': sbornik dokumentov.* Moscow, 1961.
Geronimus, A. and Orlov, V. *VKP(b) i voennoe delo v rezoliutsiakh s"ezdov i konferentsii VKP(b).* Moscow, 1928.
Golder, F.A., ed. *Documents of Russian History: 1914–1917.* New York, 1927.
Gusev, S.I. *Grazhdanskaia voina i krasnaia armiia: sbornik voenno-teoreticheskikh i voenno-politicheskikh statei (1918–1924gg.).* Moscow, 1925.
Institut Marksizma–Leninizma. *KPSS v rezoliutsiiakh i resheniiakh s"ezdov, konferentsii i plenumov TsK.* Vol. 1 (1898–1917) Eighth ed., Moscow, 1970.
Shestoi s"ezd RSDRP (bolshevikov) avgust 1917 goda: protokoly. Moscow, 1958.
"Iz dokumentov po organizatsii krasnoi armii (dokumentyi)". *Krasnyi Arkhiv* (1937) 81:147–52.
Kakurin, N.E., ed. *Razlozheni armii v 1917 gody.* Moscow, 1925.
Keirin-Markus, M.B. "O polozhenii Armii nakanune oktiabria (doneseniia kommissarov vremennogo pravitel'stva i komandirov voinskikh chastei deistvuiushchei armii)". *Istoricheskii Arkhiv.* (1957) 6:35–60.
Konovalov, V.I., ed. *Revoliutsionnoe dvizhenie v armii v gody pervoi russkoi*

revoliutsii: sbornik statei. Moscow, 1955.

Mamai, N.P. et al., eds. *V.I. Lenin o voine, armii i voennoi nauke*. 2 Vols. Moscow, 1958.

Pozner, S.M. *Pervaia boevaia organizatsiia bol'shevikov, 1905–1907gg.: stati, vospominaniia i dokumenty*. Moscow, 1934.

Rabinovich, S.E. *Vserossiiskaia voennaia konferentsiia bol'shevikov 1917g. (sbornik materialov)*. Moscow, 1931.

Revoliutsiia i RKP(b) v materialakh i dokumentakh. 7 Vols. Moscow, 1925–1927.

Sharmanov, V.G., ed. *Stroitel'stvo krasnoi armii (Sbornik statei k s"ezdu sovetov)*. Moscow, 1919.

———. *Zhizn' krasnoi armii: kratkii sbornik statei k s"ezdy sovetov (pod redaktsiei voennogo komissara)*. Moscow, 1919.

Sidorov, A.L., ed. *Revoliutsionnoe dvizhenie v armii i na flote v gody pervoi mirovoi voiny, 1914–fevral' 1917. Sbornik dokumentov*. Moscow, 1966.

———. et al., eds. *Velikaia oktiabr'skaia sotsialisticheskaia revoliutsiia: dokumenty i materialy*.

"Verkhovnoe komandovanie v pervye dni revoliutsii". *Arkhiv Russkoi Revoliutsii* (1925) 16: 279–90.

Zeman, Z.A.B., ed. *Germany and the Revolution in Russia, 1915–1918: Documents from German Archives*. London, 1958.

V. MEMOIRS AND DIARIES

Alekseev, A. "V petrogradskoi 'voenke' v 1917g". *Krasnaia Letopis'* (1926) 1(16):74–6.

Antonov-Ovseenko, V.A. "Parizhskie pis'ma". *Novyi Mir* 1964, No. 11.

———. *V semnadtsatom godu*. Moscow, 1933.

Berzin, R.I. *Etapyi v stroitel'stve krasnoi armii*. Khar'kov, 1920.

Bonch-Bruevich, V.D. *Na boevykh postakh fevral'skoi i oktiabr'soi revoliutsii*. Second ed. Moscow, 1931.

Blagonravov, G.I. "Oktiabr'skie dni v petropavlovskoi kreposti". *Proletarskaia Revoliutsiia*, (1922) 4:24–52.

Dashkevich, P.V. "Ts. O. partii v. oktiabr'skie dni". *Krasnaia Letopis'* (1933) 1 (52):101–5.

Drezen, A.K. "Petrogradskii garnizon v iiule i avguste 1917g". *Krasnaia Letopis'* (1927) 3(24):191–223.

Elov, B. "Rol' petrogradskogo garnizona v oktiabr'skie dni". *Krasnaia Letopis'* (1923) 6:98–136.

Eremeev, K., "Epizody oktiabr'skikh dnei". *Pravda*. 31 Aug. 1927. 97 (3729): 3–4.

Fleer, M. "Rabochaia krasnaia gvardiia v fevral'skuiu revoliutsiiu". *Krasnaia Letopis'* (1926) 1(16):23–43.

Fomin, V. "S"ezd deputatov armii i tyla zapadnogo fronta v aprele 1917g". *Proletarskaia Revoliutsiia* (1927) 4 (63):164–80.

Gavrilov, I. "Krasnaia gvardiia v vyborgskom raione". *Krasnaia Letopis'* (1926) 6(21):93–102.

Gordienko, I. "V kronshtadte v 1917g". *Krasnaia Letopis'* (1926) 1(16):45.

Haupt, Georges and Marie, Jean-Jacques, eds. *Makers of the Russian Revolution: Biographies of Bolshevik Leaders*. Ithaca, 1974.

Il'in-Zhenevskii, A.F. "Iiulskie dni 1917g. v petrograde". *Krasnaia Letopis'* (1926) 3(18):43–57.

———. "Nakanune oktiabria". *Krasnaia Letopis'* (1927) 4(19):5–26.

———. "Vystuplennie polkov v petrograde v iiul'skie dni 1917g". *Krasnaia Letopis'*

Selected Bibliography

(1929) 3(30):105–19.

Kaiurov, V.N. "Iz istorii krasnoi gvardii vyborgskogo raiona v 1917g". *Proletarskaia Revoliutsiia* (1927) 10(69):224–37.

Kedrov, M. "Vserossiiskaia konferentsiia voennykh organizatsii RSDRP(b) 17–23 Iiuniia (30 Iiuniia–6 Iiuliia) 1917 goda". *Proletarskaia Revoliutsiia* (1927) 6(65):216–31.

Khokhriakov, A. "Iz zhizn petrogradskogo garnizona v 1917g". *Krasnaia Letopis'* (1926) 2(17):29–50.

Kirsanova, I.I. "Permskaia voennaia organizatsiia RSDRP 1906–1908gg". *Istoricheskii Arkhiv* (1959) 2:164–8.

Kolbin, I. "Kronshtadt ot fevraliia do kornilovskikh dnei". *Krasnaia Letopis'* (1927) 2(23):136–7.

Lianin, I.M. "Iz vospominanii byvshego nachal'nika krasnoi gvardii 1-go gorodskogo raiona petrograda". *Istoriia proletariata SSSR*. (1932) 11:91–100.

Lozovskii, A. "Kak my izdavali vo vremia voiny internatsionalistski gazety v parizhe". *Pechat' i revoliutsiia* (1923) 5.

Lunacharsky, A.V. *Revolutionary Silhouettes*. London, 1967.

Lur'e, M.L. "Iz istorii petrogradskoi krasnoi gvardii v 1917g". *Krasnaia Letopis'* (1932) 5:50–1, 6:256–65.

———. "Oktiabr'skaia konferentsiia krasnoi gvardii vyborgskogo raiona". *Bor'ba Klassov* (1932) 11–12: 299–312.

Malakhovskii, V. *Iz istorii krasnoi gvardii*. Leningrad, 1925.

———. "Kak sozdavalas' rabochaia krasnaia gvardiia – zadachi izucheniia istorii krasnoi gvardii". *Proletarskaia Revoliutsiia* (1929) 10(93):27–79.

Mitrevich, I.A. "Ot maia do oktiabria". *Krasnaia Letopis'* (1923) 6:349–55.

Mukhtar-Londarskoi, M.I. "Boevaia druzhina krasnoi gvardii putilovskogo zavoda". *Istoricheskii arkhiv* (1957) 1:205–12.

Nevskii, V.I. "Voennaia organizatsiia i oktiabrskaia revoliutsiia". *Krasnoarmeets* (1919) 10:84–144.

Piontkovskii, S. "Voenno-Revoliutsionnyi komitet v oktiabr'skie dni". *Proletarskaia Revoliutsiia* (1927) 10 (69):110–37.

Podvoiskii, N. *Krasnaia Gvardiia v oktiabr'skie dni*. Leningrad and Moscow, 1927.

———. "Ot krasnoi gvardii k krasnoi armii". *Istorik Marksist* (1938) 1:3–38.

———. "Voenaia organizatsiia bol'shevikov v oktiabr'skom vosstanii". *Leningradskaia Pravda* 17 Oct. 1927, 3; 28 Oct. 1927, 3; 12 Nov. 1927, 4.

———. "Voennia organizatsiia TsK RSDRP(b) i voenno-revoliutsionnyi komitet 1917g". *Krasnaia Letopis'* (1923) 6:64–97; 8:7–43.

Rabinovich, S.E. "Vserossiiskaia konferentsiia bol'shevistskikh voennykh organizatsii 1917g". *Krasnaia Letopis'* (1930) 5(58):105–32.

Raskol'nikov, F.F. *Kronshtadt i Piter v 1917g*. Moscow, 1925.

———. "Voenno-revoliutsionnyi komitet v pitere v oktiabre 1917g". *Pravda* 7 Nov. 1925, 255 (3186), 10.

———. "V tiur'me kerenskogo". *Proletarskaia Revoliutsiia* (1923) 10 (22):133–65.

Rostov, N. "Voznikhovenie krasnoi gvardii". *Krasnaia Nov'* Feb. 1927, 168–80.

Shaurov, I.V. "Pervaia konferentsiia voennykh i boevykh organizatsii RSDRP v noiabre 1906g". *Istoricheskii Arkhiv* (1959) 1:160–71.

Shumiatskii, I. "Shestoi s"ezd partii i rabochii klass". *V dni velikoi proletarskoi revoliutsii*. Moscow, 1937.

Smilga, I.T. *K voprosy o stroitel'stve krasnoi armii*. Moscow, 1920.

Vertzinskii, E.A. *God' revoliutsii: vospominaniia ofitsera general'nago shtaba za 1917–1918gg*. Tallin', 1929.

Zhenevskii, A. "Voennaia organizatsiia RSDRP(b) i Soldatskaia Pravda".

Leon Trotsky and the Art of Insurrection 1905–1917

Krasnaia Letopis' (1926) 1(16):57–73.
Ziv, G.A. *Trotskii: kharakteristika po lichnym vospominaniam.* New York, 1921.

VI. SECONDARY SOURCES

Akhun, M.I. and Petrov, V.A. *Bol'sheviki i armiia v 1905–1917gg.* Leningrad, 1929.
Andreev, A.M. *Sovety rabochikh i soldatskikh deputatov nakanune oktiabriia (Mart–oktiabr' 1917g.).* Moscow, 1967.
Anikeev, V.V. "K istorii petrogradskoi krasnoi gvardii". *Sovetskie arkhivy* (1966) 3:35–40.
———. "Voennyi organizatsii RSDRP(b) v 1917g". *Voprosy Istorii KPSS.* (1964) 10:12–19.
Antonov, A. "Imenemn voenno-revoliutsionnogo komiteta: iskusstvo vosstaniia". *Novyi Mir* (1957) 10:160–6.
Anweiler, Oskar. *The Soviets: The Russian Workers, Peasants and Soldiers Councils, 1905–1921.* Translated by Ruth Hein. New York, 1974.
Avrich, Paul. *The Russian Anarchists.* Princeton, 1967.
Azovtsev, N.N. *Voennye voprosy v trudakh V.I. Lenina.* Moscow, 1964.
Baker, B.G. *The Passing of the Turkish Empire in Europe.* Philadephia, 1913.
Baron, Samuel H. *Plekhanov: The Father of Russian Marxism.* Stanford, 1963.
Bastareva, L.I. *Petropavlovskaia krepost'.* Leningrad, 1965.
Beskrovnyi, L.G. et al., eds. *Bor'ba bol'shevikov za armiiu v trekh revoliutsiiakh.* Moscow, 1969.
Boucabeille, E. *La guerre interbalkanique: événements militaires et politiques survenus dans la Péninsula des Balkans jusqu'en octobre 1913.* Paris, 1913.
Bubnov, A.S. *Grazhdanskaia voina, partiia i voennoe delo.* Moscow, 1928.
Buiskii, A.A. *Voennaia podgotovka oktiabria.* Second ed. Moscow, 1930.
Burdzhalov, E.N. *Vtoraia russkaia revoliutsiia: Moskva, front, periferiia.* Moscow, 1971.
———. *Vtoraia russkaia revoliutsiia: vosstanie v petrograde.* Moscow, 1967.
Carmichael, Joel. *Trotsky: An Appreciation of his life.* New York, 1975.
Carnegie Endowment for International Peace. *Report of the International Commission to Inquire into the Causes and Conduct of the Balkan Wars.* Washington, D.C., 1914.
Carr, E.H. *The Bolshevik Revolution, 1917–1923.* 3 vols. London, 1950.
———. *The October Revolution: Before and After.* New York, 1969.
Cassavetti, D.J. *Hellas and the Balkan Wars.* New York, 1914.
Chaadaeva, O. *Armiia nakanune fevral'skoi revoliutsii.* Moscow, 1935.
———. "Kak burzhuaziia gotovilas' k oktiabriu". *Krasnyi Arkhiv* (1927) 21:218–20.
———. "Soldatskie massy petrogradskoe garnizona v podgotovke i provedenii oktiabr'skogo vooruzhennogo vosstaniia". *Istorichiskie Zapiski* (1952) 6:73–113.
Chamberlin, W.H. *The Russian Revolution.* 2 vols. New York, 1963.
Chemodanov, G.N. *Poslednie dni staroi armii.* Moscow, 1926.
Cohen, Stephen F. *Bukharin and the Bolshevik Revolution: A Political Biography, 1888–1938.* New York, 1973.
Daniels, R.V. *The Conscience of the Revolution: Communist Opposition in Soviet Russia.* Cambridge, 1960.
Delafield, R. *Report on the Art of War in Europe 1854, 1855, 1856.* Washington, D.C., 1861.
Deutscher, Isaac. *The Prophet Armed: Trotsky, 1879–1921.* New York, 1954.

Selected Bibliography

Drezen, A.K. Editor. *Bol'shevizatsiia petrogradskogo garnizona.* Leningrad, 1932.

Dykov, I.G. "Petrogradskii voenno-revoliutsionnyi komitet – boevoi bol'shevistskii shtab vooruzhennogo vosstaniia v oktiabre 1917 goda". *Voprosy Istorii* (1957) 7:17–35.

Eastman, Max. *Leon Trotsky: The Portrait of a Youth.* New York, 1925.

Erykalov, E.F. *Oktiabr'skoe vooruzhenoe vosstanie v petrograde.* Leningrad, 1966.

Feldman, Robert S. "The Russian General Staff and the June 1917 Offensive". *Soviet Studies* 19 (April 1968): 526–42.

Ferro, Marc. "The Russian Soldier in 1917: Undisciplined, Patriotic, and Revolutionary". *Slavic Review* 30 (Sept. 1971): 483–512.

Furneaux, Rupert. *The Breakfast War.* New York, 1958.

Georgievskii, G. *Ocherki po istorii krasnoi gvardii.* Moscow, 1919.

German General Staff, Military Historical Section. *The Balkan War, 1912–1913.* Berlin, 1914. Typescript translation by Harry Bell for the Army Service Schools. Fort Leavenworth, Kansas: n.d.

Getzler, Israel. *Kronstadt, 1917–1921: The Fate of a Soviet Democracy.* New York, 1983.

Golub, P. *Partiia, armiia i revoliutsiia.* Moscow, 1967.

Grazkin, D.I. "Okopnaia Pravda". *Istoricheskii Arkhiv.* (1957) 4:168–83.

Harcave, Sidney. *The Russian Revolution of 1905.* London, 1970.

Helmreich, E.C. *The Diplomacy of the Balkan Wars, 1912–1913.* Cambridge, 1938.

Heyman, N.M. "Leon Trotsky as a Military Thinker". Unpublished PhD. Thesis: Stanford University, 1972.

Howell, Philip. *The Campaign in Thrace, 1912.* London, 1913.

Iadov, A.G. "Parizhskaia emigratsiia v godu voinu". *Katorga i Ssylka* (1924) 3:7–13.

Iaroslavskii, M., ed. *Pervaia konferentsiia voennykh i boevykh organizatsii RSDRP, Noiabr' 1906g.* Moscow, 1932.

Ionov, A. *Bor'ba bol'shevistskoi partii za soldatskie massy petrogradskogo garnizona v 1917 godu.* Moscow, 1954.

Iovlev, A.M. *Bor'ba KPSS za sozdanie voennykh kadrov.* Moscow, 1960.

Johnson, James G. Jr. "The Petrograd Military-Revolutionary Committee (October–December, 1917)". Unpublished PhD. Thesis: Emory University, 1974.

Kakurin, N. *Kak srazhalas revoliutsiia.* Moscow, 1925.

——. and Iakovlev, Ia. *Razlozhenie armii v 1917g.* Moscow, 1923.

Karamysheva, L.D. *Bor'ba bol'shevikov za petrogradskii sovet (Mart–oktiabr' 1917g).* Leningrad, 1964.

Katkov, George. *Russia 1917: The February Revolution.* New York, 1967.

Kliatskin, S.M. *Na zashchite oktiabriia: organizatsiia regularnoi armii i militsionnoe stroitel'stvo v sovetskoi respublike, 1917–1920.* Moscow, 1965.

Knei-Paz, Baruch. *The Social and Political Thought of Leon Trotsky.* Oxford, 1978.

Kretov, F.D. et al. *Nekotorye voprosy strategii i taktiki partii bol'shevikov v oktiabr'skoi revoliutsii.* Moscow, 1968.

Lawton, Lancelot. "A German View of the Turkish Defeat". *Fortnightly Review.* XCIII, New Series (May 1913), 975–87.

Levy, Roger. *Trotsky.* Paris, 1920.

Liddell Hart, B.H. *The Real War, 1914–1918.* Boston, 1946.

Liebman, Marcel. *The Russian Revolution*. Trans. Arnold J. Pomerans. New York, 1970.

Lipitskii, S.V. *Voennaia deiatel'nost' TsK RKP(b), 1917–1920gg*. Moscow, 1973.

Macbean, W.A. *Handbook of the Military Forces of Russia*. London, 1898.

Medlin, Virgil D. "The Reluctant Revolutionaries: The Petrograd Soviet of Workers' and Soldiers' Deputies, 1917". Unpublished PhD. Thesis: University of Oklahoma, 1974.

Melgunov, S.P. *The Bolshevik Seizure of Power*. Ed and abridged by S.G. Pushkarev. Santa Barbara, 1972.

Mikhlin, E.I., ed. *Lenin–Partiia–Oktiabr'*. Leningrad, 1967.

Ministère de la Guerre, Etat-Major de l'Armée, Service historique. *Les Armées françaises dans la Grande Guerre*. Paris, 1922–36.

Mints, I.I. *Istoriia velikogo oktiabria*. 2 vols. Moscow, 1967.

Morozov, V.V. *Ot krasnoi gvardii k krasnoi armii*. Moscow, 1958.

Movchin, N. *Komplektovanie krasnoi armii*. Leningrad, 1926.

Mukhov, F.V. "Vserossiiskaia konferentsiia frontovykh i tylovykh voennykh organizatsii RSDRP(b)". *Voprosy Istorii KPSS* (1959) 5:86–100.

Muratov, Kh. I. *Revoliutsionneo dvizhenie v russkoi armii v 1917g*. Moscow, 1958.

Nekliudov, A.V. *Diplomatic Reminiscences Before and During the World War, 1911–1917*. London, 1920.

Nenarokov, A.P. "K voprosu o nachal'nom periode stroitel'stva krasnoi armii", in *Oktiabr' i grazhdanskaia voina v SSSR – sbornik statei k 70-letiiu Akademika I.I. Mintsa*. Moscow, 1966, 434–44.

Payne, Robert. *The Fortress*. New York, 1967.

Petrov, I.F. *Strategiia i takitika partii bol'shevikov v podgotovke pobedy oktiabr' skoi revoliutsii (Mart–oktiabr' 1917g.)*. Second ed. Moscow, 1975.

Petrov, F.N., ed. *V ogne revoliutsionnykh boev (raiony petrograda v dvukh revoliutsiiakh 1917g.) – sbornik vosspominanii starykh bol'shevikov-pitertsev*. Moscow, 1967.

Pinezhskii, E. *Krasnaia gvardiia (ocherki istorii piterskoi krasnoi gvardii, 1917g.)*. Moscow, 1929.

Pipes, Richard, ed. *Revolutionary Russia*. Cambridge, 1968.

Pozner, S., ed. *Pervaia konferentsiia voennykh i boevykh organizatsii RSDRP*. Moscow, 1932.

Rabinovich, S.E. "Bol'shevistskie voennye organizatsii v 1917g". *Proletarskaia Revoliutsiia* (1928) 6–7: 179–98.

——. *Bor'ba za armiiu v 1917g.: Ocherki partiino-politicheskoi bor'byi i rabotyi v armii v 1917 gody*. Moscow, 1930.

——. "Rabota bol'shevikov v armii v 1917g". *Voina i Revoliutsiia* (1927) 6:119–26.

Rabinowitch, Alexander. *The Bolsheviks Come to Power: The Revolution of 1917 in Petrograd*. New York, 1976.

——. *Prelude to Revolution: The Petrograd Bolsheviks and the July 1917 Uprising*. Bloomington, 1968.

Reed, John. *Ten Days that Shook the World*. New York, 1960.

Rosenberg, William G. *Liberals in the Russian Revolution: The Constitutional Democratic Party, 1917–1921*. Princeton, 1974.

Rosmer, Alfred. "Trotsky in Paris during World War II", in *Leon Trotsky: The Man and his Work*. New York, 1969.

Saul, Norman, "Fedor Raskolnikov: A 'Secondary Bolshevik'". *The Russian Review*. 32 (April 1973): 131–42.

Schurman, Jacob G. *The Balkan Wars, 1912–1913*. Princeton, 1914.

Schwartz, M.N. *Trotskii*. Berlin, 1921.

Selected Bibliography

Schwartz, S.M. *The Russian Revolution of 1905: The Workers' Movement and the Formation of Bolshevism and Menshevism.* Trans. Gertrude Vakar. Chicago, 1967.

Selznick, Philip. *The Organizational Weapon: A Study of Bolshevik Strategy.* Santa Monica, 1952.

Semenov, G. *Voennaia i boevaia rabota partii sotsialistov-revoliutsionenov za 1917–1918gg.* Berlin, 1922.

Senchakova, L.T. *Revoliutsionnoe dvizhenie v russkoi armii i flote v kontse XIX – nachale XX v. (1879–1904gg.).* Moscow, 1972.

Senn, Alfred E. *The Russian Revolution in Switzerland.* Madison, 1971.

Serge, Victor. *Vie et mort de Trotsky.* Paris, 1951.

Shatagin, N. "Vos'moi s'ezd bol'shevistskoi partii i stroitel'stvo krasnoi armii". *Voprosy Istorii* (1951) 5:3–26.

Shklovskii, V.B. *Revoliutsii i front.* Petrograd, 1921.

Smith, Irving H., ed. *Trotsky.* Englewood Cliffs, 1973.

Startsev, V.I. *Ocherki po istorii petrogradskoi krasnoi gvardii i rabochei militsii (Mart 1917–Aprel' 1918g.).* Moscow, 1965.

Stone, Norman, *The Eastern Front, 1915–1917.* New York, 1975.

Stokes, Curtis. *The Evolution of Trotsky's Theory of Revolution.* Washington, D.C., 1982.

Tarasov, E.P. *Nikolai Il'ich Podvoiskii.* Moscow, 1964.

Theen, Rolf. "The Idea of the Revolutionary State: Tkachev, Trotsky, and Lenin". *The Russian Review* 31 (Oct. 1972): 383–97.

Treadgold, Donald. *Twentieth Century Russia.* Second ed. Chicago, 1964.

Tsypkin, G.A. *Krasnaia gvardiia vo bor'be za vlast' sovetov.* Moscow, 1967.

Ulam, Adam B. *The Bolsheviks.* New York, 1965.

Valk, S.N. et al., eds. *Oktiabr'skoe vooruzhennoe vosstanie: semnadtsatyi god v petrograde.* 2 vols. Leningrad, 1967.

Ventsov, S. *Ot krasnoi gvardii k vooruzhennomu narodu.* Moscow, 1927.

Vucinich, Wayne E., ed. *The Peasant in Nineteenth-Century Russia.* Stanford, 1968.

Williams, Albert R. *Journey into Revolution: Petrograd, 1917–1918.* Chicago, 1969.

Wolfenstein, E.V. *The Revolutionary Personality.* Washington, D.C., 1966.

Index

Index

155